SHARKS

a Golden Guide® from St. Martin's Press

Written by Andrea Gibson
Illustrated by
Robin Carter/Wildlife Art Ltd.

53

St. Martin's Press ♒ New York

FOREWORD

Well-researched and written, beautifully designed and illustrated, *Sharks* is a valuable source of information for those keen to learn about sharks. Covering a range of subjects, this book highlights how magnificent and yet vulnerable sharks really are.

I am particularly pleased to note that *Sharks* exposes the myth that is *Jaws*, and confirms the fact that the most dangerous animal in our oceans is man, not sharks. As many shark populations continue to be overexploited, primarily because of the value of their fins, we are witnessing a downward spiral of shark populations, with increasing shark fin prices and an increased fishing effort.

With over 18 species of shark now on the IUCN Red List (the international register of endangered species), it is gratifying to read a book that so elegantly illustrates the variety of crucial roles that these animals play in our marine ecosystems. Sharks first appeared over 400 million years ago and thrived as the ocean's top predator until only a few decades ago, when commercial fishing pressure devastated many species and extinction began to stare many in the face.

I hope this book inspires you to become concerned about sharks. Those of us lucky enough to have observed them in their natural habitat have had inspiration enough; for those who have not, this fine book is the next best thing.
Clive James, Shark Trust Director

ISBN 0-312-30607-5   First Edition: September 2002

CONTENTS

INTRODUCTION

This book is for everyone who has ever been impressed by sharks. It is for the student interested in their biology; for divers curious about their distribution and impressed by their demeanor; and for the layperson concerned about the notorious reputation of these oceanic predators.

As well as serving as a guide to the identification of the shark families and species, this book aims to dispel media myths and misconceptions and to unravel the mystery of these quiet and powerful creatures.

Sharks also aims to educate readers as to the importance of the shark, which is so abused in today's world of exotic cuisine and overfishing. In this role we are supported by one of the few international charities dedicated to saving these magnificent creatures – the Shark Trust.

www.sharktrust.org

Established in 1997, the Shark Trust promotes the international study, management, and conservation of sharks, skates, and rays.

The Trust seeks to coordinate the efforts of other shark groups and organizations and to influence and reverse the factors which are threatening shark populations. The Trust also works with commercial fisheries, recreational sea anglers, divers, yachters, and all those who want to ensure the future survival of these fascinating but threatened animals.

Priority action promotes the effective management of sustainable fisheries, improving records on catches, landings and trade, habitat management and increasing public and private-sector awareness.

To find out more visit www.sharktrust.org

NURSE SHARK

A species of the shallow waters, spending most of the daylight hours resting on the seabed. It swims slowly, with a sinuous, eel-like motion and broad sweeps of its long tail, as it searches for crustaceans and small fish.

THRESHER SHARK

An active and powerful hunter of squid and fish, which it herds and stuns using its powerful and elongate upper tail lobe.

GREAT WHITE SHARK

Chiefly a coastal species that relies on its equal-sized tail lobes for slow cruising and high-speed sprints after its often fast-moving and agile prey.

COOKIECUTTER SHARK

A tiny but savage species, fastening its needlelike teeth on a range of prey items, from crustaceans to marlins, dolphins and larger sharks. The tail, which has broad upper and lower lobes of similar size, is ideally suited to its deep-water, active lifestyle.

PREHISTORIC SHARKS

IN THE BEGINNING

Long before dinosaurs roamed the Earth, sharks had already undergone a transformation from small, sucker-mouthed scavengers into top predators.

The first cartilaginous fish appeared more than 400 million years ago in the Silurian period of the Paleozoic era. By the Devonian period, 360 million years ago, bony and cartilaginous fish had diversified into all parts of the world. This period has often been termed the Age of Fishes.

Shark evolution is still the subject of much debate. They are poorly represented in the fossil record because their cartilaginous skeletons do not fossilize well. The knowledge we have gained comes mainly from studying fossilized teeth, which, with their covering of hardened enamel, are the main calcifying materials in a shark's body. Occasionally, body parts such as tiny fin scales are found, although these are so small that they require microscopic examination. There are a few examples of whole carcasses being preserved, but they are also rare due to the fortuitous conditions required to preserve their soft tissues.

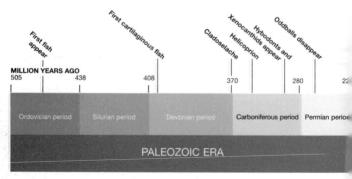

First fish appear

First cartilaginous fish

Cladoselache

Xenocanthids appear

Helicoprion

Hybodonts and

Oddballs disappear

MILLION YEARS AGO
505   438   408   370   280   22

Ordovician period   Silurian period   Devonian period   Carboniferous period   Permian period

PALEOZOIC ERA

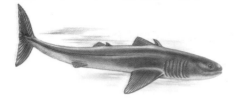

Cladoselache
5–6 feet
(1.5–1.8 m)

Sharks may be related to an extinct Paleozoic group of jawless fishes called thelodonts, which had scales similar to today's species, or they may have evolved alongside placoderms: giant jawed fishes with protective bony armor. Alternatively, they may have an entirely different ancestor.

The oldest-recognized sharklike fish is of the extinct mid-Devonian genus *Cladoselache*. *Cladoselache* was probably only 5–6 feet (1.5–1.8 m) long. It had a streamlined body with five pairs of gill slits; stiffened, paired, pectoral and pelvic fins; and long, slender jaws bearing distinctive teeth. It was probably a swift predator, actively hunting down prey items, swallowing them tail first. Although strikingly similar to today's sharks, *Cladoselache* is not thought to have given direct rise to modern sharks, mainly due to the absence of claspers (reproductive organs developed in all modern male sharks) and the fact that it did not replace its teeth as frequently as modern sharks do.

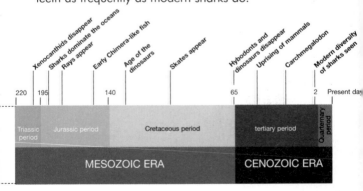

ODDBALLS

During the Carboniferous and Permian periods (370–220 mya), sharks underwent a second phase of dramatic changes, some of which were quite bizarre.

Hybodus
7½ feet (2.25 m)

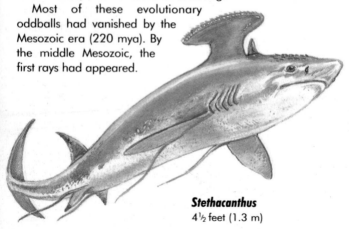

Iniopterygians, with their long, winglike pectoral fins, have been called the "missing link" between sharks and bony fish. Stethacanthids included species with elaborately modified dorsal fins that projected over their head. The teeth of *Helicoprion*, an edestid, were arranged in an outward spiral whorl, with the newest and largest teeth inside the mouth. Some of these species may have grown very large. Among the oddest were the petalodontids, which had deep, bulbous bodies, small heads, and flat teeth for crushing.

Most of these evolutionary oddballs had vanished by the Mesozoic era (220 mya). By the middle Mesozoic, the first rays had appeared.

Stethacanthus
4½ feet (1.3 m)

Most of the sharks of 220–150 mya fall into two groups. The xenacanths lived mainly in fresh water. They were long and large, with dorsal spines and tapering tails. They had a worldwide distribution until their demise 200 mya.

The second group, the hybodonts, were mostly oceanic; they dominated from 220 mya to 65 mya, when almost all other shark groups also died out.

Resembling *Cladoselache*, hybodonts had a number of advanced features linking them more closely to modern sharks. *Hybodus* had a blunt snout and an elongate body. Blunt teeth at the rear of the mouth and sharp, pointed teeth at the front suggest that *Hybodus* fed on the move.

These prehistoric predators ruled the oceans until the end of the Cretaceous period (65 mya). *Hybodus* couldn't compete with "modern sharks" and gradually disappeared at about the same time as the last dinosaurs.

Helicoprion
10 feet (3.3 m)

THE RISE OF MODERN SHARKS

With the extinction of dinosaurs and the rise of mammals, sharks underwent their third period of dramatic change. This led to the diversity of sharks we recognize today.

Since then, the diversity of the large, modern, pelagic sharks has increased with no major declines or extinctions. The oldest white shark teeth stem from this period, when two distinct lines of shark form appeared. One line had rough, serrated teeth, thought to have given rise to modern Great White Sharks; the other seems to have had a tendency to grow to enormous sizes. This group of giant sharks appears to have reached their pinnacle during the Miocene epoch (late Tertiary period), 25–10 mya. They included probably the most spectacular marine predator ever to have cruised the oceans – the giant *Carcharocles megalodon*,

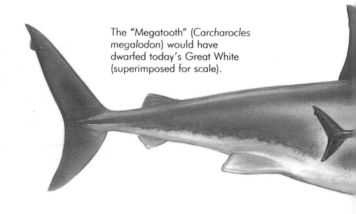

The "Megatooth" (*Carcharocles megalodon*) would have dwarfed today's Great White (superimposed for scale).

otherwise known as "Megatooth". Their fossils are found in worldwide deposits up until 3 mya. These terrifying super-predators had huge, serrated, triangular teeth around 7 inches (17.5 cm) tall and bodies 40–50 feet (12–15 m) in length.

Recent opinions are that sharks are not primitive animals as popularly thought. They actually display an advanced design with such evolutionary advantages as larger brains, specialized teeth, and extremely well-developed sensory systems, placing them with birds and mammals in terms of evolutionary complexity.

Modern studies on shark evolution make regular advances. As technologies improve, scientists are able to study minute details in fossilized shark teeth. They are now focusing on the layers laid down in tooth manufacture, and it is hoped that this will improve our understanding of sharks' evolutionary relationships.

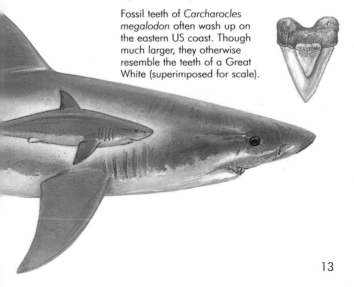

Fossil teeth of *Carcharocles megalodon* often wash up on the eastern US coast. Though much larger, they otherwise resemble the teeth of a Great White (superimposed for scale).

ANATOMY

Some basic anatomical features are common to all sharks. The mouth opens at the tip of the head or is underslung, and the pectoral and pelvic fins are paired. Some species have an anal fin, and on the back there may be one or two dorsal fins. The backbone extends into the upper tip of the tail, so the upper tail lobe is often longer than the lower. Male sharks also have claspers. These are adaptations of the pelvic fins, used in transferring sperm during copulation.

Aside from their cartilage skeleton, other features separate sharks from bony fish. They lack an opercular flap, the bony covering of the gill slits which keeps the gills hidden in most fish. In sharks, the gill slits – numbering five, six, or seven per side – are exposed.

Sharks lack a swim bladder, the mechanism in bony fish that keeps them afloat. Instead sharks have a large, oil-rich liver. In some species, such as the Blue Shark, the liver makes up to 20% of their body weight. Deep-water sharks

Unlike bony fishes, a shark has a skeleton made of cartilage. This is lighter than bone, more flexible, and just as strong.

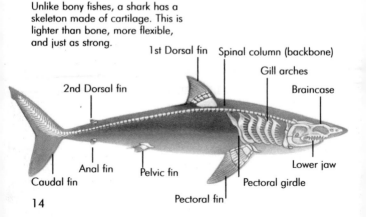

1st Dorsal fin Spinal column (backbone)

Gill arches

Braincase

2nd Dorsal fin

Anal fin Pelvic fin

Caudal fin

Lower jaw

Pectoral girdle

Pectoral fin

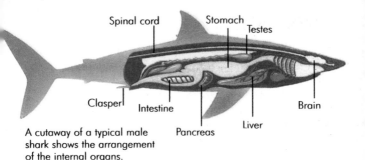

Spinal cord Stomach Testes

Clasper Intestine Pancreas Liver Brain

A cutaway of a typical male
shark shows the arrangement
of the internal organs.

need larger livers in order to control their bouyancy.

It is a myth that all sharks must keep swimming in order
to avoid drowning. Many bottom-dwelling species breathe
with a pumplike mechanism which allows them to force
water through their gills by opening and closing their
mouth. This allows oxygen uptake even when stationary.

In most sharks, tiny scales are embedded in the skin,
giving it a prickly texture. These placoid scales are thought
to have evolved from teeth and are even made of similar
materials – a pulpy cavity surrounded by dentine and
capped with enamel.

SENSES

Far from being the mindless killers of popular legend,
sharks are advanced animals with highly developed, acute
senses. These are essential navigational, communication
and hunting aids in the reduced light below the surface.

Vision

Sharks' eyes closely resemble those of other vertebrates,
even to the extent of seeing in color. Mounted on the sides
of the head, they provide a wide field of vision. In some
species an eyelid, known as the nictitating membrane, can

be flicked up to protect the eye when required. Blue Sharks, for example, are often witnessed covering their eyes with a white screen in the final moments before seizing prey in their jaws. White sharks do not have this membrane; they roll their eyes back for protection.

SMELL

Inside the nostrils are two olfactory sacs. Covering each sac is a flap of skin that channels water, and any particles suspended in it, into the nasal chamber. Here, the water flows between lamellae (small plates) lined with olfactory receptor cells. Nerve fibers lead from the cells to the brain, passing on highly detailed information about the surrounding water.

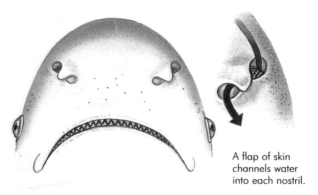

A flap of skin channels water into each nostril.

TASTE

Like the smell receptors, a shark's taste receptors can detect minute biological particles. But since the taste receptors are located inside the mouth, they come into play only when potential prey is already inside the mouth. Only then does the shark decide whether the food is palatable.

OTHER SENSES

Further senses give the shark an exceptional awareness of its surroundings. The vestibular system aids balance; the auditory system provides hearing; and electrosensory systems helps incredibly accurate location of prey.

The vestibular system is a series of fluid-filled chambers within the inner ear. This works rather like a spirit level, in that the fluid presses at various pressure points on vertical and horizontal nerve cells as the shark rolls and pitches. Using signals from the nerve cells, the shark is always aware of its body orientation relative to gravity.

Since sharks do not have external ears, they detect disturbances in the water through organs on the top of their head that lead to an inner ear.

Like all other fish (except hagfish), sharks have a lateral line system. This is a line along each flank of open pores connected to a water-filled canal system beneath the skin. Arranged along this canal are several pressure-sensitive cells known as neuromasts. The linear arrangement enables the shark to detect pressure differentials between one point and another. It can sense water movement and acceleration, and use the information to locate nearby objects, such as other, larger sharks or prey.

The lateral line system consists of pores (**A**) connected to canals (**B**) beneath the skin (**C**). Lining the canals are pressure-sensitive cells (**D**) known as neuromasts, which connect to the brain. Changes in the external water pressure are sensed by the neuromasts, which alert the shark to the presence and location of objects in the water, such as prey or predators.

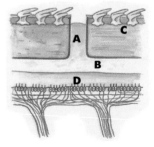

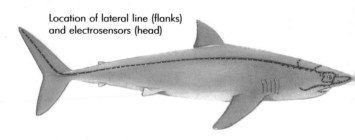

Location of lateral line (flanks) and electrosensors (head)

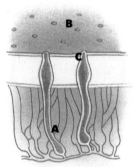

The electrosensory system is a field of organs called ampullae of Lorenzini (left). These sacs (**A**) under the skin are connected to surface pores (**B**) by way of jelly-filled canals (**C**). They detect the voltages given off by the muscular activity of other animals nearby.

Sharks have an additional sense, unique to them, which allows them to detect weak electrical voltages in the water immediately around them.

Clusters of sacs, known as the ampullae of Lorenzini, lie beneath the skin of the snout and lower jaw. From each ampulla, a canal filled with conductive jelly leads to a pore on the skin. Using this system, a shark can pick up the tiny electrical signals that are involuntarily discharged by moving prey. Signals pass from each pore to the ampullae, and onward to the central nervous system, where they form an electrical "map" of the surroundings.

This electrosensory system is ineffective at long range, but works superbly within a range of 1 foot (30 cm) or so. It enables bottom-feeding species, for example, to strike accurately at prey concealed in shallow sand.

REPRODUCTION

Sharks do not live in pairs, and mating is sometimes the only time when members of the same species come together. With their naturally aggressive tendencies, sharks show no recognizable courtship displays. Although males do tend to follow pheromone-producing females, looking for some kind of recognition prior to mating, this possibly serves only to reduce aggression once mating begins. Even so, both parties may suffer serious bites and other injuries during the act itself.

Relative to bony fish, which practice external fertilization, sharks produce few offspring. It is not unusual for a female bony fish to release millions of eggs into the water, where they are fertilized by the male's free-floating sperm. In sharks, fertilization occurs internally. The male uses his claspers to transfer sperm into the female's cloaca.

Shell gland Ovary   Uterus   Cloaca

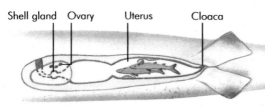

Females either lay eggs, incubate eggs internally, or retain the embryos (above) to full term of development.

A male (below) uses his claspers, a modification of the pelvic fins, to transfer sperm into the female.

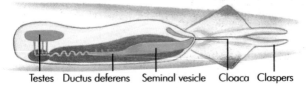

Testes   Ductus deferens   Seminal vesicle   Cloaca   Claspers

Anywhere from one to a few dozen offspring are produced. The gestation period of young sharks varies greatly, from a few months to nearly two years in the Spiny Dogfish – the longest known gestation period of any animal.

Sharks also produce their offspring at different stages in their development. There are three methods: egg-laying (oviparity), live young developed internally without a placenta (ovoviviparity) and live young developed internally with a placenta (viviparity).

OVIPARITY

Sharks that lay eggs are termed oviparous. They include the Hornsharks, Catsharks, Zebra Sharks, and Carpet Sharks. Once fertilized, the eggs are enclosed in a strong, protective casing and usually laid in shallow, sheltered areas on the seabed.

The embryo obtains all the nutrition it needs from the yolk sac within the egg case. When the yolk is fully consumed, the pup cuts its way out with the help of specialized serrated scales on its snout. The hatched pup is a perfect miniature version of the adult and is fully capable of hunting its own prey.

OVOVIVIPARITY (nonplacental vivipary)

In ovoviviparity the embryo develops internally, in a membrane in the mother's uterus. After a variable period of development, the membrane ruptures, leaving the embryo to complete development with a yolk sac still attached. This food source is fully absorbed before birth.

Tiger Sharks are ovoviviparous, and females can produce from 10 to more than 80 young, each about 27½ inches (70 cm) long. Other ovoviviparous species include the Spiny Dogfish, as well as the Wobbegongs, Angelsharks, Houndsharks, and Sevengill Sharks.

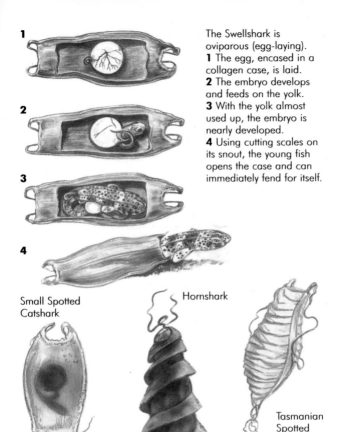

The Swellshark is oviparous (egg-laying).
1 The egg, encased in a collagen case, is laid.
2 The embryo develops and feeds on the yolk.
3 With the yolk almost used up, the embryo is nearly developed.
4 Using cutting scales on its snout, the young fish opens the case and can immediately fend for itself.

Small Spotted Catshark

Hornshark

Tasmanian Spotted Catshark

Egg cases

Egg cases may be quite elaborate in their design. Some posses long tendrils at their corners by which they become anchored to weeds and debris on the seabed. Some, such as the Hornshark's eggs, are spiral in shape, which help the egg to become tightly wedged among rocks and stones.

21

This is the embryo of a Piked Dogfish, an ovoviviparous shark. The pup develops internally, unattached to the mother, and is nourished by its egg yolk. It absorbs the yolk fully before birth, whereupon it is a fully formed pup.

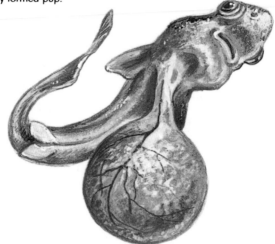

VIVIPARITY (placental vivipary)

Viviparity is broadly similar to ovoviviparity, except that in this method a placenta and an umbilical cord develop, providing a direct link between the mother and the embryo – not unlike the development of placental mammals. Hammerhead, Smoothhound, Blacktip, Silvertip, and Dusky Sharks all follow this reproductive pattern.

In viviparous species the individual egg membrane divides the uterus into separate chambers for each embryo. The cord is formed when the yolk sac depletes and fuses with the uterine wall.

This illustration shows how the embryos develop in separate chambers within the uterus. Each embryo has its own umbilical cord.

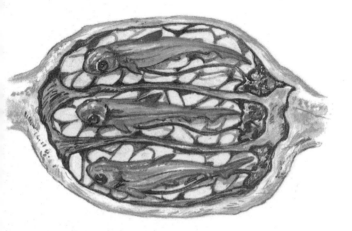

CANNIBALISM

Some shark embryos exhibit their predatory nature well before birth. They practice intra-uterine cannibalism, which means they eat each other while still inside the uterus. There are two methods: oophagy, where the developed embryos eat the remaining eggs, and embryophagy, where the embryos eat each other.

Though this sounds barbaric, it ensures that those pups that survive have the best possible chance in life right from the start. Oophagy is seen in the Mako, Great White, Basking, Porbeagle and Thresher Sharks. Embryophagy is more unusual and is only known in Sand Tiger and Gray Nurse Sharks.

WHERE SHARKS LIVE

Sharks are found in almost every aquatic environment on Earth. They are at their most common and diverse in tropical and temperate waters, especially off the coasts and ocean shelves. Sharks live wherever their main prey is most abundant, so they tend to favor coral and rocky reefs, estuaries, lagoons, open beaches, and rocky coastlines.

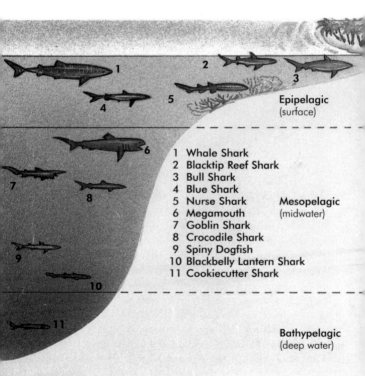

Epipelagic
(surface)

1 Whale Shark
2 Blacktip Reef Shark
3 Bull Shark
4 Blue Shark
5 Nurse Shark
6 Megamouth
7 Goblin Shark
8 Crocodile Shark
9 Spiny Dogfish
10 Blackbelly Lantern Shark
11 Cookiecutter Shark

Mesopelagic
(midwater)

Bathypelagic
(deep water)

Other popular hunting grounds are the areas where swell produces upwellings of nutrients, such as at river mouths. A few sharks are attracted to fresh water, although no species lives exclusively in fresh water. Bull Sharks are a well-known freshwater visitor and are sometimes found quite far inland. In India's city of Varanasi on the Ganges River, some 600 miles from the sea, these sharks feed on the human corpses released to the holy river.

Whatever their distribution, sharks fall into two groups: open-water species or bottom-dwellers. Open-water sharks often favor a particular level in the water column. Those living near the surface are called "epipelagic"; those of the middle water zone are "mesopelagic"; and deep-water species are "bathypelagic."

TROPICAL SHARKS

Sharks are considered tropical if they usually live in waters warmer than 70° F (21° C). Open-water tropical species, tend to follow seasonally changing water temperatures, and as a result can migrate over huge distances. The larger, warm-water species are found in all of the world's tropical oceans. They include Tiger, Bull, Oceanic Whitetip, Blacktip, Great Hammerhead, and Whale Sharks.

Bottom-dwelling, warm-water sharks tend to have much smaller ranges. They spend most of their time lying on the seabed and move only to feed or breed. Most are well camouflaged and are usually less than 6 feet (1.8 m) long. Typical examples are the Carpetsharks and Angelsharks. Larger bottom-dwellers include the Zebra and Nurse Sharks.

TEMPERATE SHARKS

Temperate species live in waters of 50–70° F (10–21° C). Like their tropical counterparts, active temperate species follow fluctuations in water temperatures. In the winter months, they congregate around the equator, and in summer, they disperse from it into cooler waters. These sharks, which also display a circumglobal distribution, include the Mako, Great White, Blue, and Basking Sharks. Of these, the Blue Shark probably ranges the most widely.

As well as frequenting the higher latitudes of the world, temperate sharks can also be found in the deeper, cooler waters of tropical zones. Examples include the Spiny Dogfish, the Tope Shark, and the Houndsharks.

Bottom-dwelling temperate sharks are usually less than 6 feet (1.8 m) in length. They tend to be sluggish and move little from their birth site. This tends to mean that their distribution is restricted. Examples include the Angelsharks, Sawsharks, Hornsharks, and Catsharks.

COLD-WATER SPECIES

Cold-water sharks inhabit waters less than 50° F (10° C). Many live close to Arctic and Antarctic waters, while others live in the very deep parts of the temperate or tropical seas. One amazing species, the Greenland or Sleeper Shark, even lurks beneath the north polar icecap. Few species inhabit the colder depths below 6,000 feet (1,830 m), the exception being the Portuguese and Velvet Dogfishes, which live in utter darkness at depths of up to 12,000 feet (3,660 m)!

Other active cold-water species includes the Sixgill and Sevengill Sharks, Frilled Shark, False Catshark and Goblin Shark. The smaller cold-water sharks live at depths over 900 feet (275 m) and include many of the Dogfish.

The bottom-dwelling, cold-water sharks are all small species, with restricted distributions and little dispersal from their birth site during their lifetime. Two groups in particular fit this description – the Prickly Sharks, and the Catsharks of the genus Apristurus.

FEEDING

Sharks owe much of their success to the way they feed. A huge leap forward in their evolution came with the freeing of the upper jaw from the skull. This adjustment gave the mouth more flexibility, allowing sharks to protrude their jaws and hunt more effectively. This action can be seen on the right. When the shark is not feeding, the upper jaw is tucked against the skull (**1**). During an attack (**2**), the snout rises and the lower jaw is thrust forward to grip the prey. The upper jaw then protrudes (**3**) and comes down hard on the prey. The upper teeth then "saw" out a chunk of flesh.

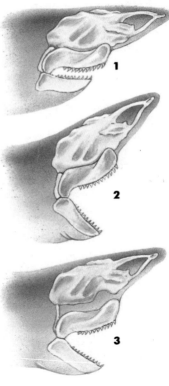

DIET

A sharks diet depends on its size, dentition, and preference, but their menus may include anything from plankton, bony fish, sea urchins, shrimp, squid, octopus, turtles, penguins and other seabirds to large marine mammals such as seals, sea lions, dolphins and even other sharks.

27

1 **2**

TEETH

Most sharks have sharp, cutting teeth, although a species' dentition depends on its diet. Teeth are regularly produced and shed throughout the shark's life. Some may produce 30,000 teeth in a lifetime, which accounts for their abundance in the fossil record!

Shark teeth are arranged in rows on the jaws, with each new row appearing posteriorly, so that the teeth move forward in the mouth as each new row is produced. This tooth "conveyor belt" is highly effective, because it allows blunt and broken teeth to be replaced and allows the shark to continue hunting. It also ensures that new teeth develop at the shark's growth rate. It has recently been discovered that some sharks begin teething in the uterus or the egg case.

Shark teeth are extremely diverse. The Gummy Shark's flattened, cuspless teeth help crush prey. The primitive Goblin Shark's teeth are used to impale. Great Whites and Tiger Sharks, which attack large prey, have serrated teeth that tear away chunks of flesh.

Gummy Shark   Goblin Shark   Great White Shark   Tiger Shark

3

The Great White shark's protrusible jaws give it a fearsome bite. The shark attacks at high speed (**1**). The head rises and the jaws open (**2**). In the final instant (**3**) the jaws protrude and the eyeballs roll back.

HUNTING

Since the evolution of the modern shark form, a number of feeding mechanisms and techniques have developed.

FILTER FEEDERS

The Whale, Basking, and Megamouth Sharks have developed a filter-feeding mechanism. Having greatly reduced teeth, these sharks possess modified gills with gill rakers, an adaptation for straining plankton from water. Like teeth, the gill rakers are shed and replaced throughout the animal's life.

HUNTERS THAT LURE PREY

In habitats where prey is hard to spot and harder still to pursue, such as the dark waters of deep oceans, it pays for an animal to resort to trickery. The odd-looking Cookiecutter Shark, a deep-water species, uses the bioluminescence trick to lure prey. On its flanks are photophores, organs containing symbiotic bacteria that can generate flashes of light. These photophores mimic similar organs in phosphorescent krill and squid. When a suitable animal approaches, such as a seal or a dolphin, expecting a mouthful of krill, the Cookiecutter flits forward and tears a plug of flesh from the would-be predator.

The Megamouth Shark is thought to have a glowing lining inside its mouth, which attracts krill. In order to feed, all it needs to do is to keep its huge mouth open.

29

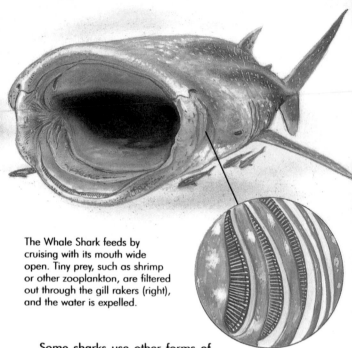

The Whale Shark feeds by cruising with its mouth wide open. Tiny prey, such as shrimp or other zooplankton, are filtered out through the gill rakers (right), and the water is expelled.

Some sharks use other forms of deception to lure prey. The Nurse Shark rests on its pectoral fins on the seabed and keeps still. The cavity below its body looks like an atractive shelter to certain small fish in search of cover, and before long they wander into the deadly trap.

Wobbegong Sharks rely on their deceptive body plan. The flaps of skin around the mouth break up their outline, while their color and markings resemble the seabed. They, too, lie and wait for prey to come within range.

Angelsharks have a slightly different tactic. They like to bury themselves in a sandy or muddy seabed. When suitable prey comes close, they explode from hiding with their mouth agape. The Swellshark has a simple but devastating feeding technique reminiscent of Anglerfishes. It opens its mouth, drawing in water and sucking in any small fish that get too close.

The Angelshark is a sneaky predator. It lies still on the seabed, hidden by a scattering of sand scuffed up with the pectoral fins. When prey passes overhead, the shark bursts upward to attack.

DEFENSIVE BEHAVIOR

Although formidable, sharks still need protection. The smaller species are particularly vulnerable, especially to larger sharks. Many have physical defenses, such as the dorsal fin spines of the Hornsharks. Another example is the

31

Swellshark, which can suck in copious amounts of water to inflate its body and appear larger and much more menacing than it really is. If this does not deter its aggressor, the shark can use the same technique to lodge its body firmly among rocks, preventing removal.

Most peple with first-hand experience of a shark attack claim to have received no warning that an attack was imminent. However, it is thought that sharks will give some warning before they attack. The Gray Reef Shark, for example, swims in exaggerated fashion, arching its back and lowering its pectoral fins. Another indicator of a shark's annoyance is tail-flicking. In this display, the shark swims at its aggressor and turns suddenly at the last minute, flicking its tail to whip the water with a loud crack. Divers should be aware of these signals.

The Gray Reef Shark may give a warning display before attacking. This includes (**1**) arching the back, (**2**) lowering the pectoral fins and (**3**) flicking the tail from side to side.

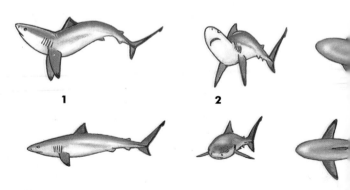

1

2

The juvenile Zebra Shark is well camouflaged against predators. Its stripes break up its body outline and conceals it on the seabed.

CAMOUFLAGE

For most sharks, defense is a matter of hiding. The mottled skin colors and patterns of bottom-dwelling species help them to blend in with their habitat. Wobbegongs and Angelsharks can be especially hard to find.

Some sharks have quite vivid coloration at birth and for some time after. Zebra Shark pups, for example, sport the dramatic stripes of their namesake, which provides excellent cryptic protection when they are at their most vulnerable stage in life.

Like many fish of the open waters, most free-swimming sharks have countershading camouflage. They have a pale-colored underside, so that when they are seen from below they blend with the sunlit surface waters. Darker upperparts make them difficult to distinguish from the ocean depths when viewed from above.

3

WHEN SHARKS ATTACK

For some people the very thought of swimming with sharks sends shivers down the spine. In truth, sharks pose no more danger than a pet dog.

Most shark incidents are simply a case of mistaken identity. Our aquatic hobbies – swimming in warm, shallow waters, diving in deep coral seas and wreck sites – puts us in their world. These environments just also happen to be inhabited by some of the largest and potentially most dangerous shark species.

Shark attacks are on the rise, but the statistics are misleading. It is not that sharks are growing more accustomed to human flesh; the fact is, we are encroaching more often on their environment. This intrusion places us at risk if we do not respect them.

Shark attacks, or more correctly, incidents, can usually be avoided. It is only natural to panic if a shark swims too close or brushes against your skin. However, the shark is merely assessing a new and unfamiliar presence in its realm.

If you can remain calm and aware, you may observe how the shark uses its olfactory and electrosensory systems to interpret its surroundings. It is constantly on the lookout for danger, as well as for food, and the signals it picks up will tell it whether or not you pose a threat. In response, the shark will either display signals as described on page 32, or it may simply retreat. If the shark is taunted or

Great White Shark attacks on surfers are usually a case of mistaken identity. We do look remarkably like sea lions from their point of view!

threatened it may well attack if these signals are ignored.

Most Great White Shark attacks on surfers usually happen because the surfer is mistaken for a seal. And since they bite to taste food, the mistake is not discovered until its is too late. At that point a shark usually spits out its human mouthful. It is important to keep matters in proportion – there were fewer than 550 shark attacks on humans during the 1990s, and only a small percentage of these were fatal.

CONSERVATION

Having survived millions of years and witnessed the extinction of many other prehistoric creatures, sharks themselves are now under greater threat than ever before. Man is responsible for the deaths of more than 100 million sharks each year – that's one shark dying every three seconds, every year.

The greatest threat facing many sharks today is the despicable practice of "finning". This involves the dorsal fins being cut from the live shark, which is then dumped back into the sea, to die a slow and painful death. Unbelievably, fins are only used as an ingredient for soup. International organizations are campaigning to end this truly barbaric practice. Sharks are also commercially fished for the oil in their livers, known as squalene oil. This has numerous commercial uses, but is largely used for cosmetic purposes.

Sharks are fished for many commercial uses, including soup (fins), lip gloss, vitamin A, and skin cream (liver oil).

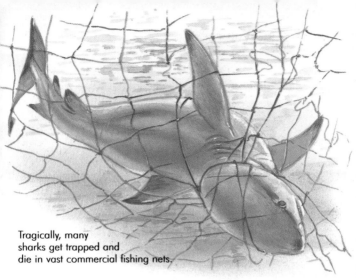

Tragically, many sharks get trapped and die in vast commercial fishing nets.

Many sharks are also fished for their meat. Again, however, overfishing of some species has caused populations to collapse. With their slow rate of reproduction, many species of shark cannot recover from intensive commercial fishing practices.

Sharks, along with dolphins, turtles, and birds, are also caught in vast fishing nets. Longline fishing is also having devastating effects on shark numbers. Recreational anglers pose a minor threat, seeking the spectacular teeth and jaws for trophies. Pollution, too, is poisoning the sharks' ocean habitat.

In 2000, 11 species of shark were listed as threatened. By late 2001 this had risen to 18. International cooperation has helped enormously; Great White and Sand Tiger Sharks, for example, are now protected in some parts of the world. But numbers, which had declined rapidly, will take years to recover.

CLASSIFYING SHARKS

Scientists, known as taxonomists, divide shark species which are closely related and physically similar into distinct groups, or "orders". This system of classification is based primarily on their physical characteristics, with the main dividing feature being the presence or absence of an anal fin. The shape of their body and the number of dorsal fins are secondary dividing characteristics. This simple method of taxonomy is easy to understand when represented by an identification tree, as shown on the right.

The total number of shark species is updated and revised all the time. The current view is that there are over 420 types of shark. They are classified into eight orders and further subdivided into thirty-four families. The following pages describe each of these orders and their family members, and include illustrations and information on their representative or most commonly recognized species.

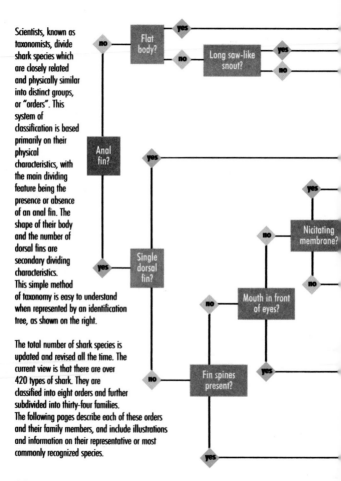

Squatiniformes
    Squatinidae (Angelsharks)
Pristiophoriformes
    Pristiophoridae (Sawsharks)
Squaliformes
    Squalidae (Dogfish Sharks)
    Echinorhinidae (Bramble Sharks)
    Centrophoridae (Gulper Dogfish)
    Etmopteridae (Lanternsharks)
    Somniosidae (Sleeper Sharks)
    Oxynotidae (Rough Sharks)
    Dalatiidae (Kitefin Sharks)
Hexanchiformes
    Chlamydoselachidae (Frilled Sharks)
    Hexanchidae (Sixgill, Sevengill, and Cow Sharks)
Carcharhiniformes
    Scyliorhinidae (Catsharks)
    Proscylliidae (Finback Catsharks)
    Pseudotriakidae (False Catsharks)
    Leptochariidae (Barbeled Houndsharks)
    Hemigaleidae (Weasel Sharks)
    Triakidae (Smoothhound Sharks)
    Carcharhinidae (Requiem or Whaler Sharks)
    Sphyrnidae (Hammerhead Sharks)
Lamniformes
    Odontaspididae (Sandtiger Sharks)
    Pseudocarchariidae (Crocodile Sharks)
    Mitsukurinidae (Goblin Sharks)
    Megachasmidae (Megamouth Sharks)
    Alopiidae (Thresher Sharks)
    Cetorhinidae (Basking Sharks)
    Lamnidae (Mackerel Sharks)
Orectolobiformes
    Parascyllidae (Collared Carpetsharks)
    Brachaeluridae (Blind Sharks)
    Orectolobidae (Wobbegongs and Carpet Sharks)
    Hemiscyllidae (Bamboo and Epaulette Sharks)
    Stegostomatidae (Zebra Sharks)
    Ginglymostomatidae (Nurse Sharks)
    Rhincodontidae (Whale Sharks)
Heterondontiformes
    Heterondontidae (Horn or Bullhead Sharks)

The primitive order Hexanchiformes contains two families: the Chlamydoselachidae (Frilled Shark) and the Hexanchidae (Sevengill and Sixgill Sharks).

Hexanchiformes have one spineless dorsal fin, an anal fin, and six or seven gill openings (most sharks have five). They occur worldwide in deep waters. All species are ovoviviparous.

Chlamydoselachidae is an ancient family. The sole member, the Frilled Shark, lives in the coldest depths. Its head bears resemblance to the early armored fishes, and it may be a direct descendant of *Cladoselache*.

FRILLED SHARK *Chlamydoselachus anguineus*

Also known as the Eel Shark, this species grows to 6½ feet (2 m). It is reasonably common on the bottom and upper slopes of continental shelves, at depths of 300–4,250 feet (120–1,300 m). It is occasionally seen at the surface.

The first of the six gill slits almost encircles the head, like a collar. The common name derives from the frilly margins of skin around the gills. The snout is short and rounded, and the lower jaw is long.

The Frilled Shark probably hunts squid and fish. After a gestation period of 1–2 years, the female gives birth to 8 to 12 pups, each measuring 16 inches (40 cm).

The Frilled Shark is thought to be primitive on account of its dentition, having tricusped teeth, which are highly unusual among sharks.

There are more than 300 teeth, arranged in rows in the jaws.

41

The family **Hexanchidae** contains four species – two with seven gills per side, two with six. They are all heavy-bodied, with one dorsal fin and an underslung mouth. They are not oceanic, preferring shallower offshore and coastal waters.

BROADNOSE SEVENGILL *Notorynchus cepedianus*

Also called the Spotted Sevengill Shark, this species grows to 7 feet (2.2 m) in the female, 5 feet (1.5 m) in the male. Widespread though not abundant, the Sevengill favors temperate waters around continental shelves, usually keeping to depths of about 450 feet (135 m).

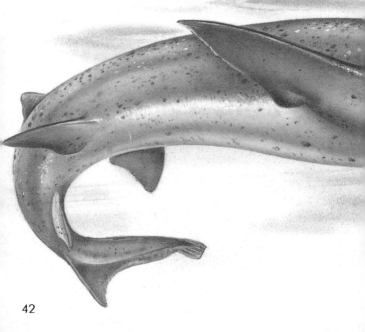

Other than the seven gills, distinguishing features are a broad head and short, rounded snout. The mouth is wide and the eyes small. Coloration is silvery-gray to brownish, with dark- and pale-speckled flanks and a pale belly. There is the characteristic single dorsal fin and an anal fin. The young Broadnose Sevengill has whitish margins on its fins.

This large shark is a powerful swimmer. A voracious and indiscriminate hunter, it preys on other sharks and rays, as well as squid, bony fishes, seals, crustaceans, and carrion.

The ovoviviparous females bear litters of up to 82 pups, which measure 16–18 inches (40–45 cm) at birth.

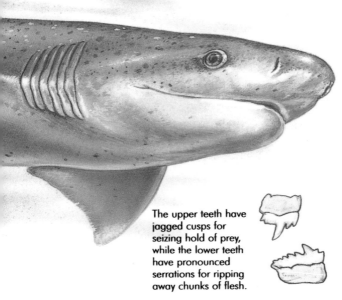

The upper teeth have jagged cusps for seizing hold of prey, while the lower teeth have pronounced serrations for ripping away chunks of flesh.

BLUNTNOSE SIXGILL *Hexanchus griseus*

Also called the Sixgill Shark or Bull Shark, this species grows to a maximum of 15¾ feet (4.8 m).

A worldwide coast-dweller in northern temperate and cold waters, the Bluntnose Sixgill is also found around oceanic islands as far south as northern parts of tropical seas. It favors shelves and slopes at depths of 650–5,400 feet (200–1,650 m). Younger sharks prefer shallower waters but stay close to the seabed. Adults usually keep to dimly lit and dark waters. They can be found at the surface in the open ocean, especially at night.

The relatively small teeth are set in rows of six. The uppers are pointed for grabbing prey, while the lowers are serrated for sawing off chunks of flesh.

The Bluntnose Sixgill is deep-bodied. The dorsal fin is located toward the tail. The small eyes are set wide on the broad head. The body is long and powerful, and a huge tail propels this hunter in pursuit of its prey, which includes other sharks, rays, dolphins, cod, and billfishes. Smaller prey includes squid, crab, shrimp, and herring.

Females reach sexual maturity at about 14 feet (4.3 m) and give birth to as many as 100 young measuring 24–28 inches (60–70 cm). The species is fished commercially for its oil and meat.

This is one of four six-gilled shark species. The others are the Frilled Shark, the Sixgill Sawshark, and the Big-eye Sixgill Shark. The latter is in the same family as the Bluntnose; the Big-eye Sixgill can be told apart by its more slender body and (not surprisingly) its larger eyes. The two species also differ in dentition: The Big-eye Sixgill has five rows of teeth (six in the Bluntnose), and they are sawlike in appearance.

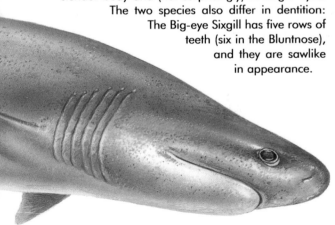

The Squaliformes (Dogfish Sharks) is the second-largest shark order, with seven families and at least 110 species.

Squaliforms possess two dorsal fins, sometimes bearing spines, but have no anal fin. All have five gills, a cylindrical body, and short, often powerful jaws beneath a long snout. They are found in all oceans to depths of 20,000 feet (6,000m). All are ovoviviparous.

The family **Echinorhinidae** (Bramble Sharks) contains two species: the Bramble and the slightly larger Prickly Shark. Both are stout-bodied, with a flattened head and two spineless dorsal fins set far back. The Bramble Shark is the more common of the two, with the Prickly Shark confined to the Pacific Ocean.

BRAMBLE SHARK

Echinorhinus brucus
Also called the Spinous Shark, this species grows to 10 feet (3.1 m) in length. It ranges widely in tropical and temperate waters of the Atlantic, Indian, and Pacific Oceans and associated seas. Favoring deep continental shelves and upper slopes at 1,300–3,000 feet (400–900 m) depth, it sometimes enters water as shallow as 36 feet (11 m).

Denticles (tooth-like scales) in the skin account for this shark's name. The flag-like tail is a key identifying feature.

In the Bramble Shark, the first dorsal fin is situated above the pelvic fins. Another key feature is the large, thick, unnotched tail fin. The oval eyes are large, and the snout is short and pointed. Small spiracles (air inlets) lie behind the eyes. The head is flattened, and the rough skin is purplish to gray with paler undersides.

Both species prey on a variety of seabed life, from the egg cases of other sharks and chimeras to bony fish, crustaceans, cephalopods (like squid and octopus), and smaller sharks. The female Bramble Shark bears up to 30 young measuring 12–36 inches (30–90 cm) in length.

The family **Squalidae** has the same collective common name as the order: Dogfish Sharks. It is a large family of more than 70 diverse species, ranging from the tiny to the huge. These species are typically slender, with a cylindrical or slightly flattened body. Most have two dorsal fins lacking spines. The range of this family is probably greater than any other, extending from Arctic to tropical waters.

SHORTNOSE SPURDOG *Squalus megalops*

Also called the Bluntnose Spiny Dogfish or Dogshark, this petite species grows to a length of just 28 inches (71 cm). A deepwater shark, it is confined mainly to the Indo-Pacific, from southern African to Australian waters, at depths of 100–2,460 feet (30–750 m). It favors the bottoms of outer continental shelves and upper slopes. Younger Spurdogs keep to open waters until able to defend themselves.

A short, angular snout houses a small mouth. There are two spined dorsal fins, the posterior of the two having a spine as long as the fin. There is no anal fin. The unmarked skin is a coppery-gray color above and paler below.

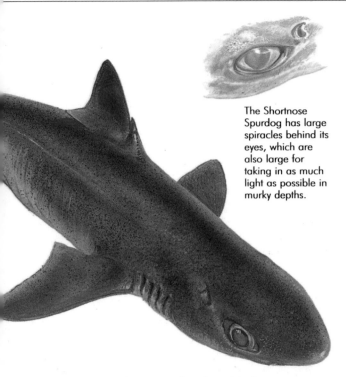

The Shortnose Spurdog has large spiracles behind its eyes, which are also large for taking in as much light as possible in murky depths.

Shortnose Spurdogs are often found in large same-sex gatherings. They prey mainly on bony fishes, crustaceans, cephalopods and other elasmobranchs. After a gestation period of almost two years, females usually bear between two and four young in a litter. The newborn measure 8–9½ inches (20–24 cm).

Along with many other members of its family, this shark is heavily fished for human consumption.

49

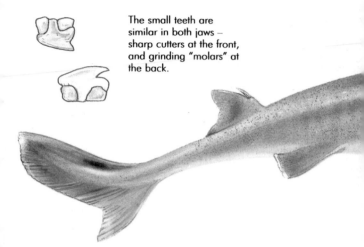

The small teeth are similar in both jaws — sharp cutters at the front, and grinding "molars" at the back.

PIKED DOGFISH *Squalus acanthias*

This is a well-known species, as attested by its many alternative names. It is also known as the Codshark, Thornshark, or Skittledog, and as the Spiny, White Spotted, Spotted Spiny, or Victorian Spotted Dogfish.

The Piked Dogfish may grow to 5 feet (1.5 m) in length. It is native to the North Atlantic, the Mediterranean Sea, and the Pacific. Favoring cold-temperate waters around coasts and continental shelves, it ranges from the shallows to depths of 2,600 feet (800 m). It migrates both latitudinally and within the water column to remain in the colder zone at temperatures of 45–60 °F (7–15 °C).

A long, slender shark, the Piked Dogfish has two spined dorsal fins, the second being larger than the first. Each spine is capable of delivering a mild venom to attackers.

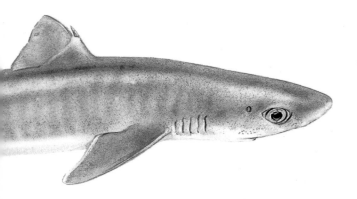

The pectoral, pelvic, and tail fins have pale posterior edging. There is no anal fin. The large spiracle behind the large eye is an identifying feature of this species. The body is a pale to mid-gray above and paler below, with white spots along the upper half of the body. The snout is long and pointed, and the teeth are sharp and bladelike.

The Piked Dogfish is possibly the most abundant shark in the world. Individuals swim together in very large schools and are often found in shallower waters in spring months, moving to deeper waters in the winter months.

A slow swimmer, the Piked Dogfish is an active predator. It takes a wide variety of small fishes, as well as krill, cephalopods, and other invertebrates.

Females bear between 2 and 11 pups, measuring 8–12 inches (20–30 cm). Birthing usually occurs every two years after the longest gestation period known for any shark – up to 24 months.

Another heavily overfished species, the Piked Dogfish is a threatened species; it is taken mainly for its flesh.

The family **Centrophoridae** contains two genera – *Centrophorus* (11 species) and *Deania* (four identified species). They inhabit warm-temperate and tropical waters of the Atlantic, Indian, and Pacific Oceans. Both dorsal fins have a grooved spine, and the lower teeth are larger than those on the upper jaw.

BIRDBEAK DOGFISH *Deania calcea*

This species, also known as the Thompson's, Brier, or Shovelnosed Shark, can grow to 45 inches (113 cm). A deepwater bottom-dweller, the Birdbeak is found at depths of 1,300–3,000 feet (400–900 m). It favors continental and insular slopes in the eastern Atlantic and Pacific Oceans.

A long, flattened, and blunt-tipped snout accounts for the Birdbeak's name. The eyes are large, and the dorsal fins bear characteristic grooved spines. Body color ranges from pale to dark gray or dark brown. The female bears

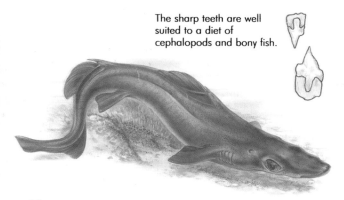

The sharp teeth are well suited to a diet of cephalopods and bony fish.

6 to 12 pups per litter, measuring 12 inches (30 cm) at birth.

The Birdbeak is not a danger to humans. It is fished for its liver oil, which is especially rich, having a high squalene content on account of the water depths it favors.

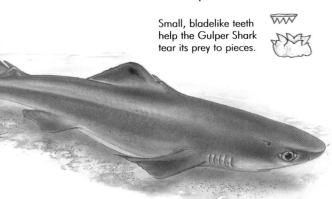

Small, bladelike teeth help the Gulper Shark tear its prey to pieces.

GULPER DOGFISH *Centrophorus granulosus*

Also called the Gulper Shark, this species grows to 6 feet (1.8 m). It frequents the warmer waters of the Atlantic and the Mediterranean, staying near the seabed at depths of up to 1,640 feet (500 m).

Adults are usually a rather dull olive-gray to brown with no markings, though juveniles may have paler fin margins. Large spiracles open behind the big green and highly reflective eyes. Prey includes lanternfish, hake, and other deepwater bony fish, as well as squid. Few reproduction details are known, except that newborns measure up to 15 inches (40 cm).

53

The Lanternshark family, **Etmopteridae,** contains 26 species. Bioluminescent (light-producing) organs on their bellies help conceal these sharks when viewed from below by predators or prey. The light also attracts prey, such as crustaceans. The Dwarf Lanternshark is the smallest living shark – it grows no longer than 8 inches (20 cm)!

HOOKTOOTH DOGFISH *Auleola nigra*
This small shark, up to 24 inches (60 cm) long, has been found only in the Pacific off South America, where it is thought to live on or near the seabed at depths of 300–2,000 feet (90–600 m).

The Hooktooth Dogfish has a dark body with white-rimmed fin tips. It has large eyes, rounded pectoral fins, and no anal fin. The diet is probably bony fish. The female is ovoviviparous and bears three or more pups in a litter.

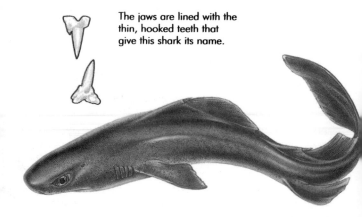

The jaws are lined with the thin, hooked teeth that give this shark its name.

BLACKBELLY LANTERNSHARK

Etmopterus lucifer

Also known as the Lucifer Shark, this species can reach a length of 18 inches (45 cm). A bottom-dweller, it has been found in warmer waters within its range off East Asia, southern Africa, Australia, and South America, but prefers colder depths of up to 3,300 feet (1,000 m).

This shark uses its light organs to mimic phosphorescent algae and attract hungry squid and krill to their doom.

This slender, dark shark has two spined dorsal fins and no anal fin. Large eyes, spiracles, and nostrils no doubt come in useful in its dark environment. The species can be distinguished from other Lanternsharks by the arrangement of its skin denticles (toothlike scales) and by its fins and markings. It is probably ovoviviparous like its relatives.

55

The 16 species in the **Somniosidae** family (Sleeper Sharks) have low dorsal fins and small pectoral and pelvic fins. They include one of the largest of all predatory fish, the Greenland Shark, which can exceed 21 feet (6.4 m).

PORTUGUESE DOGFISH *Centroscymnus coelolepis*

Growing to 4 feet (1.2 m), this shark is a slope-dweller of the eastern Atlantic, Mediterranean, and western Pacific. It prefers the cool, dark waters at 900–12,000 feet (270–3,675 m) – the deepest recorded for any shark.

Long yet stocky, it has two small dorsal fins with tiny spines. The adult is dark brown, the juvenile a very dark blue. Large denticles cover the skin.

The diet is mostly squid and seabed fish, but may also include seals or dolphins. There are usually 15 pups in a litter, measuring 12 inches (30 cm) in length.

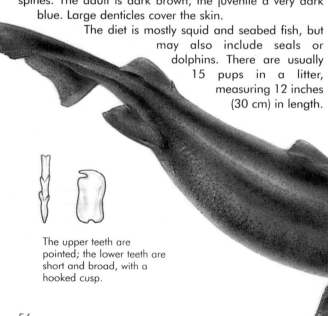

The upper teeth are pointed; the lower teeth are short and broad, with a hooked cusp.

LITTLE SLEEPER *Somniosus rostratus*

The Little Sleeper Shark can grow to a maximum length of 4½ feet (1.4 m). This rather rare species is distributed around the northeastern Atlantic Ocean and the Mediterranean Sea. It is thought to be a cold, open-water shark, staying close to the seabed at depths below about 1,300 feet (400 m).

The body is slender with two low, spineless dorsal fins. The tail has a small keel, there is no anal fin, and the pelvic fins are close to the tail. The snout is short and blunt, and behind the small eyes are prominent spiracles. The dark gray or olive-brown color is typical of a seabed-dweller.

Contrary to its common name this is an active predator. It has fairly large teeth for devouring seabed invertebrates and fish. The female Sleeper Shark is ovoviviparous. She gives birth to as many as 18 pups, measuring 8–12 inches (20–30 cm).

The members of the family **Oxynotidae** are known as the Roughsharks because of the texture of their skin. They include some of the most extraordinary-looking sharks of all. There are five species: the Prickly Dogfish, Caribbean Roughshark, Angular Roughshark, Japanese Roughshark, and Sailfin Roughshark.

PRICKLY DOGFISH *Oxynotus bruniensis*
This species reaches a length of 2½ feet (75 cm). It usually occurs in temperate waters off southern Australia and New Zealand at depths of 165–1,640 feet (54–540 m).

With its deep, plump body and sail-like, spined dorsal fins, the Prickly Dogfish is instantly recognizable. The body seems almost triangular in shape, with a flattened head and tapering snout. Behind the fairly large eyes are obvious spiracles. The underslung mouth is small, but has visible, fleshy lips.

The jaws in the short snout bear small, sharp teeth that are more pointed in the upper than in the lower jaw. There is a strong overall resemblance to the Cookiecutter Shark (page 63).

58

Denticles (toothlike scales) pepper the pinkish-brown hide, accounting for the species' common name. The fin margins of the dorsal, pectoral, and pelvic fins are often white and sometimes translucent. A visible ridge runs the length of the belly region, there is no anal fin, and the upper tail lobe is dramatically longer than the lower lobe.

This cumbersome shark is believed to live a rather sedentary life, feeding on bottom-dwelling invertebrates and bony fishes.

The prickly dogfish is ovoviviparous, with the female bearing as many as seven pups in a litter. The newborns measure 4 inches (10 cm). Little else is known about this deep-dwelling enigma.

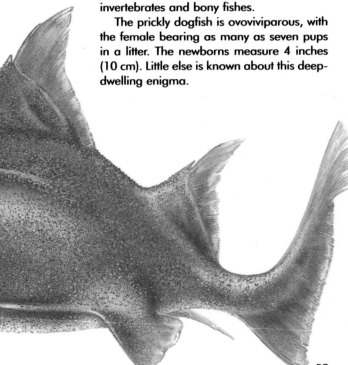

Members of the family **Dalatiidae** (Kitefin Sharks) have rough skin and two dorsal fins with spines. They occur in tropical and temperate seas to depths of 2,300 feet (700 m).

The Kitefin Shark described here is the sole member of its genus. The other genera are *Euprotomicrus* (Pygmy Shark, one species); *Euprotomicroides* (Taillight Shark, one species); *Heteroscymnoides* (Longnose Pygmy Shark, one species), *Isistius* (Cookiecutters, three species), *Mollisquama* (Softskin Dogfish, one species), and *Squaliolus* (Pygmy Sharks, two species).

KITEFIN SHARK *Dalatias licha*

Females of the species grow to 5½ feet (1.6 m), while males reach only 4 feet (90 cm). The kitefin shark occurs in the eastern Atlantic (including the western Mediterranean), the Pacific, and the western Indian Ocean. It rises to depths of about 130 feet (40 m), but prefers the seabed at depths of 650–5,900 feet (200–1,800 m).

A mid-sized shark, it has a short, rounded snout and thick lips. There is no anal fin, and the tail fin has a short lower lobe. The pelvic and pectoral fins are short and rounded. Skin coloration may vary from brownish-gray to black, though blotchy pigmentation is sometimes evident.

The Kitefin Shark is a powerful and heavy-jawed species. It preys on various bony fish, including hake, lanternfish, and skate, as well as smaller sharks from such genera as *Squalus*, *Centrophorus*, and *Etmopterus*. Squid and crustaceans are also eaten.

This solitary-living species is ovoviviparous, giving birth to between 10 and 16 young measuring 12 inches (30 cm).

The Kitefin is a small, but powerfully jawed shark. The upper teeth are small and hooked, while the large lower teeth have serrated edges.

The genus *Isistius* contains three species: the Cookiecutter Shark (*I. brasiliensis*), the China Sea Cookiecutter (*I. labialis*), and the Largetooth Cookiecutter (*I. plutodus*). Their common name gives a clue to the method by which they feed. All three species have sucking lips and jaws full of bladelike teeth. Whales, seals, tuna, billfishes, and even Great White Sharks feel the bite of these small sea-devils.

Bioluminescent organs on the body of a Cookiecutter lure other creatures. When a suitable target swims within striking range, the Cookiecutter attaches its mouth firmly to the victim, then violently twists its lower jaw to gouge out a "plug" of flesh. The bite leaves a perfectly round wound as though made by a pastry-cutter.

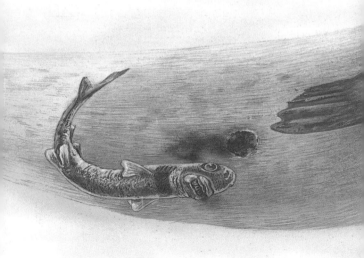

COOKIECUTTER SHARK *Isistius brasiliensis*

Also known as the Cigar Shark or Luminous Shark, this species grows to 20 inches (50 cm) in length. It occurs in oceanic waters, from the surface to depths of 3,280 feet (1,000 m). Though found worldwide, it is seldom seen.

The shark is usually dark brown above and paler below, though its light organs can give off a greenish glow. Behind the gills is a "collar" of darker pigment. The dorsal fins are set close together, far back toward the tail. There is no anal fin, and the pectoral fins are small. The snout is short, bulbous, and broadly conical, with large eyes and prominent spiracles behind them. Nothing is known of the Cookiecutter's breeding habits.

The lower jaws contain rows of 25 to 31 large, triangular teeth used for gouging plugs of flesh. The upper teeth, not used for gouging, are considerably smaller.

The order Pristiophoriformes (Sawsharks) comprises one family, which contains five species in two genera. All but one species, the Sixgill Sawshark, have five pairs of gill slits.

These harmless bottom-dwellers have a long, flattened snout with sharp, protruding teeth. Touch-sensitive barbels on the snout are used to probe the seabed for food. All species are ovoviviparous.

COMMON SAWSHARK *Pristiophorus cirratus*

Also known as the Longnose Sawshark, this species grows to 4½ feet (1.5 m). Found in temperate waters off southern Australia, it favors muddy or sandy slopes and continental shelves to depths of 1,000 feet (30 m).

The body is flattened, with large pectoral fins. The dorsal fins lack spines. The yellowish skin is patterned with brownish markings and studded with denticles.

The snout makes up almost 30 percent of the total body length. The shark drags its long barbels over the seabed in search of small bony fish, crustaceans, and squid.

Sawsharks breed in the colder winter months, and the female bears up to 22 pups after a gestation of 12 months. The newborns measure 11–15 inches (28–38 cm).

The Common Sawshark is harmless to humans, though the snout can inflict wounds if carelessly handled. This species is fished for its reportedly delicious flesh.

When the Sawshark senses likely prey, it sweeps its snout from side to side to stir up the seabed sediment and expose its quarry.

65

The order Squatiniformes comprises 18 species of Angelshark, all in the genus *Squatina*. Small and raylike in shape, they can be distinguished from rays by their pectoral fins, which do not connect to the head, and their lack of an anal fin. They spend the day buried under sand, at depths of 4,260 feet (1,300 m). At night they stay buried in order to ambush prey. All are ovoviviparous.

PACIFIC ANGELSHARK *Squatina californica*

Also known as the Monkfish or Monk Shark, this species grows to a maximum length of 5 feet (1.4 m). It is found in waters of the eastern Pacific, from Alaska south to Mexico and from Ecuador south to southern Chile at depths of 10–300 feet (3–90 m). The Pacific Angelshark lurks in rocky reefs and on sandy seabeds. During the day its large eyes alone betray its location.

This shark is a master of the ambush. It bursts from the seabed to grab prey in its protrusible jaws and small, spiky teeth. The flurry of motion stirs up sediment from the seabed.

66

The skin is colored a mottled gray-brown and matches the seabed. The broad, rounded pectoral fins are free from the body at the margins, while the gill slits are on the undersurface. The small dorsal and tail fins are all set far back on the body.

Activity usually peaks around dusk and midnight, when the Angelshark lies in wait to ambush unsuspecting octopus, squid, crustaceans, and other prey.

The Pacific Angelshark was once common, but numbers are dwindling as a result of overfishing.

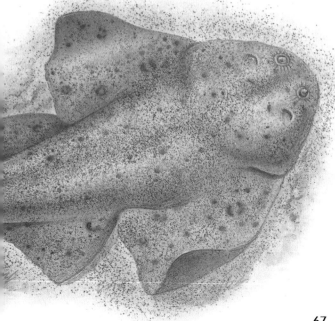

The order Heterodontiformes comprises a single family: the Heterodontidae, known as the Bullhead or Hornsharks. The single genus, *Heterodontus*, contains eight species. This genus name, from the Greek language, means "mixed teeth" and describes the varied dentition of the Bullheads.

All are bottom-dwellers and are the only sharks to have an anal fin as well as spines on both dorsal fins. They have a rather blunt, piglike snout. All females are oviparous, laying eggs in a tough, spiral-shaped egg case.

The large pectoral fins may be used for "walking" along the seabed, and the fin spines are effective defenses against predatory fishes and other, larger sharks.

CRESTED BULLHEAD SHARK

Heterodontas galeatus

The Crested Bullhead grows to 5 feet (1.5 m). It lives off the eastern coast of Australia and is a bottom-dweller, ranging from the intertidal zone to depths of about 300 feet (90 m). It stays close to rocky and coral reefs and seagrass beds.

The body is grayish, with a brownish collar and dark patches on the head, back, and tail. Similar in looks to the Port Jackson Shark (page 71), the Crested Bullhead is distinguished by its blunt snout and tall "eyebrows." Its markings are also less defined. The fins are large and rounded, and both dorsal fins have spines.

Favorite prey includes sea urchins, mollusks, crustaceans, and small fishes. The female lays spiral egg cases with long, slender tendrils. The young, measuring 6½ inches (17 cm) in length, hatch about five months later.

Heterodontid sharks have distinctive piglike snouts and rows of small, sharp teeth.

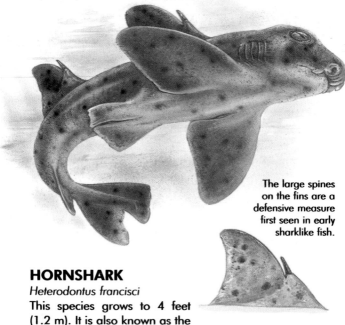

The large spines on the fins are a defensive measure first seen in early sharklike fish.

HORNSHARK

Heterodontus francisci
This species grows to 4 feet (1.2 m). It is also known as the Bullhead or California Hornshark, and occurs from central California to Baja. Adults range from cool intertidal zones to depths of 450 feet (140 m) on rocky reefs or kelp beds. Juveniles tend to stay in sandy shallows until large enough to defend themselves.

The Hornshark has spotted upperparts, high eye-crests, and a piglike snout. A sluggish shark, it sometimes "walks" on the seabed on its paddlelike pectoral fins. It eats mostly sea urchins, as well as worms, crabs, anemones, and small fishes. The female lays spiral eggs, which hatch after 7–9 months. The fully formed young are 6 inches (15 cm) long.

PORT JACKSON SHARK *Heterodontus portusjacksoni*

Also known as the Oystercrusher or Tabbigaw, this species grows to 4 feet (1.2 m) in length. A shark of southern Australian waters, it lives on or near rocky beds to depths of around 560 feet (170 m).

Dark saddlelike markings across the body and onto the fins make the Port Jackson Shark easy to identify. Both dorsal fins have large spines, thought to be venomous.

The diet consists mostly of sea urchins, mollusks, crustaceans, and fishes. The shark forages mainly at night, and usually spends the daytime hiding among rocks.

The female lays up to 16 brown egg cases. They have a spiral of four or five turns, and short tendrils at the apex. She uses her fins to push the cases into rock crevices. The young sharks hatch in the fall, measuring 9 inches (23 cm).

A look inside the mouth shows the many rows of crushing teeth, which move forward and are shed when worn.

The order Orectolobiformes (Carpetsharks) comprises 37 species in seven families. These long, sinuous sharks have a piglike snout and a mouth connected to the nostrils by grooves. Short barbels on the inner margins of the nostrils help the sharks feel for prey on the seabed. All species live in warm or tropical waters of moderate depths. They have two spineless dorsal fins and an anal fin.

The two genera in the family **Parascyllidae** (Collared Carpetsharks) are *Cirrhoscyllium*, containing three species, and *Parascyllium*, containing four. These sharks live in the western Pacific. They are all small, with large, protruding, catlike eyes. The first dorsal fin is set far back on the body, beginning behind the pelvic fins.

Next to the large, grooved nostrils can be seen the sensitive barbels with which Collared Carpetsharks feel for prey on the murky seabed.

72

NECKLACE CARPETSHARK *Parascyllium variolatum*

This striking-looking species is also known as the Varied Carpetshark, Varied Catshark, or Southern Carpetshark. It grows to a length of 3 feet (91 cm). It favors continental shelves off southwestern and southern Australia, to depths of 600 feet (180 m).

A long, thin shark with a tubular body and a large, vertically flattened head, it has two dorsal fins of uniform size, as well as an anal fin and an elongate tail fin. The species derives its pretty name from the dark band around its neck, which is also covered in dense white spots. The barbels are short and hang from under the snout.

Active at night, the Necklace Carpetshark preys on seabed crustaceans on rocky reefs and seagrass meadows. The dark skin, spattered with white spots, provides superb camouflage in starlit waters.

Nothing is known about this shark's reproductive habits, except that they are oviparous.

The second family of the Orectolobiformes order is the **Brachaeluridae**, or Blind Sharks. It comprises two species: the true Blind Shark (*Brachaelurus waddi*) and the Bluegray Carpetshark (*Heteroscyllium colcloughi*). Both are common in Australia's warm waters. They are small sharks found in the intertidal zone to depths of 360 feet (110 m).

Each shark has two spineless dorsal fins, nasal grooves and quite long barbels which protrude from the nostrils. There is a notch in the chin, and large spiracles open below the eyes.

BLIND SHARK *Brachaelurus waddi*

The Blind Shark or Brown Catshark grows to 4 feet (1.2 m). It is not in fact blind, but earned the name from fishermen through its habit of rolling back its eyes when distressed. It is found on rocky shores off south-central eastern Australia, from tidal pools to depths of 300 feet (90 m).

The brown, pale-flecked skin is covered with small denticles. The dorsal fins are of similar size and close-set. The broad head has a longish, blunt snout.

This is a nocturnal shark that often shelters under ledges and caves by day. At night it forages for fish and invertebrates, crushing them with its broad teeth. Often entering water barely deep enough to cover its body, it is one of the few sharks capable of staying out of water for some time. The ovoviviparous female bears seven or eight pups, 7 inches (18 cm) long, in late spring or early summer.

The Blind Shark has long nasal barbels and grooves connecting the nose to the mouth, enabling the shark to detect underwater scents.

The third Carpetshark family, **Orectolobidae**, contains six species of Wobbegong in three genera – *Eucrossorhinus* (one species), *Orectolobus* (four species) and *Sutorectus* (one species). All live in the western South Pacific.

The body is flattened, and the wide mouth is adorned with long barbels and flaps of skin. There are five gill slits per side. There are two dorsal fins of similar size near the tail. A groove leads from the nostrils to the mouth.

Wobbegongs live on the seabed on coral or rocky reefs. By day they ambush prey opportunistically, and actively stalk at night. All are ovoviviparous, bearing large litters.

ORNATE WOBBEGONG *Orectolobus ornatus*

Also called the Banded or Gulf Wobbegong, this species grows to 9½ feet (2.9 m). It is found in Indonesia, Papua New Guinea, Australia and Japan, in intertidal waters to depths of 100 feet (30 m).

The Wobbegong's skin is beautifully marked with dark and pale bands and marbled with blotches, breaking up the body outline against the mottled rocks or table corals on which it rests by day. Against a

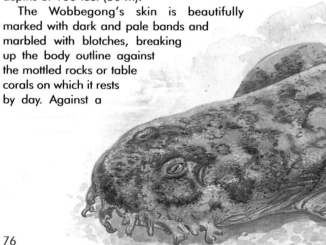

matching background, the shark is almost impossible to spot. The frilly barbels and nasal flaps around its mouth add to the camouflage.

Always ready to snap up a meal, the Wobbegong eats bony fish, sharks and rays, cephalopods, and any crustaceans that come within range.

The female gives birth to litters of usually 12 pups or more, each 8 inches (20 cm) long.

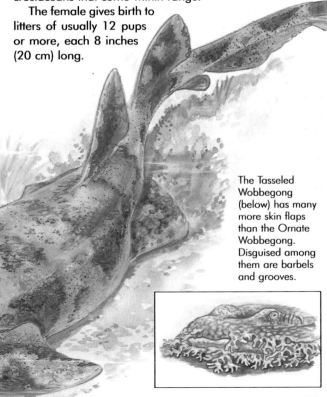

The Tasseled Wobbegong (below) has many more skin flaps than the Ornate Wobbegong. Disguised among them are barbels and grooves.

The **Hemiscyllidae** family of Long-tailed Carpetsharks contains five species of Epaulette Shark (*Hemiscyllium* spp.) and seven species of Bamboo Shark (*Chiloscyllium* spp).

They live in continental Indo-Pacific waters. Muscular pectoral and pelvic fins enable them to "walk" about the coral and rock fissures of their seabed haunts. All have five gill slits per side, a small mouth, and nasal grooves. There are two spineless dorsal fins, an anal fin, and a long tail stock. Most species lay eggs.

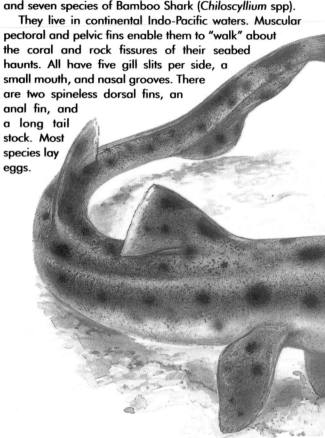

EPAULETTE SHARK *Hemiscyllium ocellatum*

Also known as the Ocellated Bamboo Shark, this species grows to a length of 3⅓ feet (1 m). It lives in reefs off Australia and New Guinea to depths of 30 feet (9 m).

The snout has a rounded tip, and the large eyes have slit-shaped pupils. The orange body is spotted black, with a large, black, white-ringed spot by the pectoral fins.

This shark is active at night and solitary. The female lays usually two oval egg cases, which have a tendril at the apex for anchoring the case to coral and rocks while the pup develops. The new hatchling measures 6 inches (15 cm).

This shark preys mostly on invertebrates. Its mouth drops and protrudes to scoop worms from the seabed or suck shrimps and crabs from crevices.

The family known as **Ginglymostomatidae** (Nurse Sharks) contains two species: the true Nurse Shark (*Ginglymostoma cirratum*) and the Tawny Nurse Shark (*Nebrius ferrugineus*).

These sharks can grow to a considerable size. They have in common two large, spineless dorsal fins, an anal fin, and a relatively short tail stock terminating in an elongated fin. The head is broad and the body fairly stout, neither having any markings.

Distributed worldwide, Nurse Sharks are also common, especially in the Caribbean. They are bottom-dwellers, ranging from the intertidal zone to depths of 230 feet (70 m). Both species have nasal grooves and visible barbels, and small spiracles are located behind the eyes. They are night-active, preying on seabed life.

Long barbels hang from the grooved nares (nostril openings). The nurse shark uses them to feel the seabed for likely prey.

NURSE SHARK *Ginglymostoma cirratum*

The Nurse Shark typically grows to 10 feet (3 m), but can reach 14 feet (4.3 m). Frequenting shallow tropical parts of the Atlantic and eastern Pacific, it is perhaps the most commonly spotted shark in reef and inshore waters to depths of 160 feet (50 m).

On the broad head, long barbels extend from the grooved nasal openings. Small spiracles open behind and below each eye. The skin is a plain gray or brown, once the dark spots of the juvenile stage have faded.

The shark hunts at night for crustaceans, sea urchins, and slow-moving fish, using its barbels to probe the seabed. It also preys on octopus and squid. The ovoviviparous female produces 20 to 30 pups, measuring about 12 inches (30 cm) long, in the spring and summer.

The family **Stegostomatidae** contains one species, the Zebra Shark. With beautiful markings and a characteristic body shape, it is an unmistakable shark.

ZEBRA SHARK *Stegostoma varium*

Also known as the Leopard or Blind Shark, this species grows to 11½ feet (4 m). Common in the tropical West Pacific, it ranges from moderate shallows to depths of 100 feet (30 m). It favors coral or rocky reefs or sandy beds. The slender, flexible tail is almost as long as the body. The head is broad and rounded, and the snout bears short barbels and large spiracles behind the eyes. Of the five gill slits per side, the fourth and fifth overlap above the pectoral fin. The two dorsal fins are close-set near the base of the tail, and the pectoral fins are large and rounded. In the adult shark, pronounced keels extend from behind the head almost to the tail tip.

The zebra name derives from the juvenile, which has yellow stripes on its dark body. These fade to the adult's "leopard-print" pattern. The true Leopard Shark (page 122) of the cold eastern Pacific has very different coloring.

Zebra sharks are fairly sluggish by day. At night they prey on bivalve mollusks, sea snails, crabs, and fish.

The female lays large, round eggs with anchor threads. The hatchlings measure 8 inches (24 cm). This shark is heavily fished for the table and for use as fishmeal.

As a juvenile the zebra sharks stripes are distinctive.

The family **Rhincodontidae** is represented by a single surviving record-breaking species. This is the world's largest fish: the Whale Shark.

WHALE SHARK *Rhincodon typus*

This giant typically grows to 18–35 feet (5.5–10.5 m) in length, but may well reach 65 feet (20 m). It is found in all tropical and subtropical oceans, both in open waters and near coasts. It is a common sight at the surface.

The body is patterned with alternating white stripes and spots over a dark blue-gray. Keels extend the length of the upper body and flanks. The huge mouth opens to the width of the head, and the tail fin has two strong lobes.

This shark is primarily a filter feeder, although they will take small fish. It cruises near the surface, taking plankton and fish ranging in size from anchovies to sardines. The planktonic strainers are internal spongy filters at the gill arches, which retain prey in the mouth. As it feeds, the shark pumps water through the gills to maximize oxygen

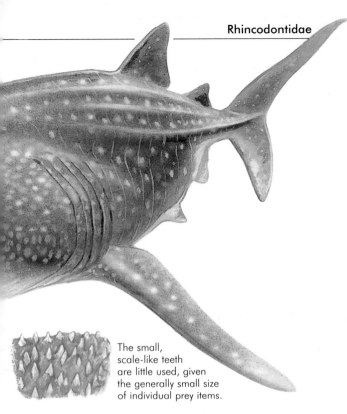

The small,
scale-like teeth
are little used, given
the generally small size
of individual prey items.

supply. When feeding, the shark turns its head from side to side and gapes its mouth up to 30 times a minute. The gulps suck in huge drafts of water, which are later exhaled at the same rate from the gill slits. Fast feeding is especially effective amidst a planktonic bloom or a shoal of small fish.

The female is ovoviviparous, giving birth to hundreds of hatched young per litter. Exploited for its flesh, liver oil, and fins, the Whale Shark is now a threatened species.

The order Lamniformes contains what most of us think of as "typical" sharks. Its members are called Mackerel Sharks on account of the tail fin, which looks like that of the mackerel. The order contains 16 species in seven families and is represented in marine environments worldwide.

Lamniforms typically have five gill slits and two spineless dorsal fins. The jaw is advanced, with an underslung mouth hinged well behind the eyes. The upper jaw teeth are unusual in that those in the front of the mouth are large, leading to medium-size teeth at the side, and smaller teeth at the back.

All Lamniformes are ovoviviparous. They range in size from 3⅓ feet (1 m) to the 33 feet (10 m) of the huge basking shark – the world's second-largest fish.

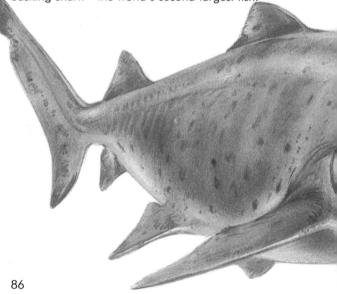

The family **Odontaspididae**, which some experts divide in two, contains four species in two genera.

SAND TIGER SHARK *Carcharias taurus*

Also known as the Gray Nurse or Ragged-tooth Shark, the Sand Tiger grows to 10½ feet (3.2 m). It lives in warm Atlantic and Indo-Pacific waters, ranging from sandy shallows and reefs to depths of 650 feet (200 m).

This shark can hang motionless in the water, owing its neutral buoyancy to a large liver and the apparently unique habit of gulping air at the surface. It preys on sharks, rays, squid, bony fishes, lobsters, and crabs. Despite their vicious appearance they are not a menace to man. The female bears one or two pups, measuring 3½ feet (1.2 m).

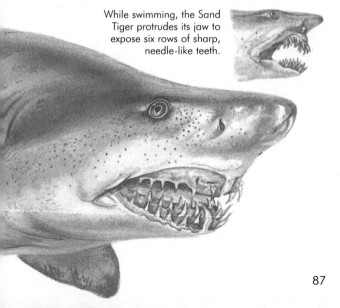

While swimming, the Sand Tiger protrudes its jaw to expose six rows of sharp, needle-like teeth.

The lamniform family **Mitsukurinidae** contains a sole, bizarre-looking species: the Goblin Shark.

GOBLIN SHARK *Mitsukurina owstoni*

The Goblin or Elfin Shark grows to a length of 12 feet (3.6 m).

This species, thought to have become extinct 100 million years ago, was "rediscovered" in the 1890s. It lives in the cold, dark depths of the Atlantic, the western Indian Ocean, and the western Pacific. It stays near the bottom at depths of about 1,200 feet (366 m).

The long, gray, flabby body has a pinkish tinge on account of the proximity of blood vessels to the skin surface. The eyes are tiny. The anal fin is broadly rounded, and the tail is

The Goblin Shark keeps its jaws retracted most of the time, concealing the sharp, needlelike front teeth.

almost as long as the body. The nostrils open in front of the mouth, and the snout has a flattened tip. This extraordinary snout is thought to contain effective electrosensors that help the shark detect prey in the darkness.

Though rather sluggish, the Goblin Shark is an efficient predator, capable of engulfing prey in a single bite. The protrusible jaws are lined at the front with sharp, needle-like teeth. Small molarlike teeth at the back grind up the crustaceans, small fish, and squid that the shark eats.

The Goblin Shark is thought to be ovoviviparous.

The Mackeral Shark family **Pseudocarchariidae** contains a sole species, the Crocodile Shark. It is closely related to the Sand Tiger Shark, with which it was once classified in the genus *Odontaspis*. Since 1973, the Crocodile Shark has been given a family of its own in recognition of its unique features. A rare and little-known species, it is now regarded as a primitive relative of the Megamouth Shark.

CROCODILE SHARK *Pseudocarcharias kamoharai*

The Crocodile Shark, which grows to a length of 3½ feet (1.2 m), is distributed in subtropical and tropical zones of the Atlantic and Indo-Pacific. It is found in coastal, insular, and oceanic waters, where it is most often seen far from land. The shark is thought to visit surface waters at night, returning toward the seabed during daylight hours.

The distinctive streamlined, cylindrical body bears two spineless dorsal fins, the first markedly larger than the second. The pectoral and pelvic fins are broad-tipped with a rounded forward edge, and there is a small anal fin. The tail fin is asymmetrical with a large, notched upper lobe and a smaller, sickle-shaped lower lobe.

The body is gray to dark brown above and occasionally sports dark blotches below. The fins have narrow white margins. The large eyes are a feature of this species. The snout is moderately long and pointed, and the large underslung jaws can be protruded some distance.

Buoyed by a liver packed with rich oil, the Crocodile Shark is a highly active, fast-swimming predator. Its dentition, jaw structure, and powerful tail section are ideal for the pursuit of large prey, which

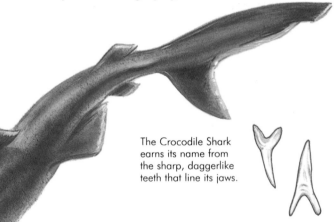

The Crocodile Shark earns its name from the sharp, daggerlike teeth that line its jaws.

includes bony fish such as lanternfish and bristlemouths, as well as squid and various crustaceans.

The female is ovoviviparous. Like many members of the lamniform order, this species also displays intra-uterine cannibalism: within each chamber of the uterus, two pups eat the other fetuses. Up to four pups are eventually born – two from each uterus. They measure 16 inches (40 cm).

The family **Megachasmidae** contains only one species, known to date, from only 15 individuals. The first Megamouth Shark was found in 1976 off the Hawaiian island of Oahu. Considered the most primitive lamniform, the Megamouth has independently evolved the filter-feeding mechanism seen also in the Whale Shark and Basking Shark.

MEGAMOUTH SHARK *Megachasma pelagios*

This large species, which grows to 17 feet (5.5 m), is known from the Indian, Pacific, and Atlantic Oceans. It is thought to range widely, though the large, flabby body and soft fins make it a poor swimmer. An inhabitant of the open seas, it is thought to migrate daily between the surface and the deepwater column, rising at night and sinking by day within an overall depth range of 50–500 feet (15–150 m).

This shark is named for its bulbous head and huge mouth, which may exceed 3⅓ feet (1 m) in width. There are five gill slits per side. The pectoral fins

are large, the anal fin small, and the two dorsal fins also small. The overall upper body coloration is blackish-brown, while the undersides of the body and fins are white. The front of the snout sports a white band.

The Megamouth is a gentle plankton-feeder. Its palate is thought to have an iridescent lining that lures krill and other luminous crustaceans. The shark "inhales" the krill by protruding its jaws and gaping its mouth, then closes and retracts the mouth, expelling water from the gills. Observations suggest this shark makes daily trips towards the depths of the ocean.

The female shark is believed to be ovoviviparous. Her embryos probably eat any spare eggs before hatching, which is termed oophagy.

The Megamouth has about 50 rows of small teeth, although the forward three rows alone are thought to be functional.

93

The Thresher Sharks, family **Alopiidae**, are unmistakable. In each species, the upper tail-fin lobe is greatly elongated. This feature is used as a keel for a strong downward thrust, and as a "whip" for slapping the water to stun prey fish. Threshers also have distinctive gills, with the hindmost slits opening over the pectoral fins. There are three species: the Pelagic Thresher (*Alopias pelagicus*), Bigeye Thresher (*A. superciliosus*), and Common Thresher (described below).

COMMON THRESHER SHARK *Alopias vulpinus*

Also called the Thintail Thresher, Whiptail, or Fox Shark, the Common Thresher grows to 18 feet (5.5 m). A highly migratory species, it occurs in the Atlantic and Indo-Pacific, from surface waters to 1,150 feet (350 m) depths. Adults roam open waters, while juveniles favor coastal shallows.

The snout is blunt, with large eyes. The first dorsal fin is much larger than the second. The pectoral fins are large and paddlelike. The body is dark-blue gray to blackish above and white below.

Prey includes schooling fish, such as mackerel, bluefish, and lanternfish, as well as crustaceans and cephalopods. The female gives birth to four to six hatched young 4–5 feet (1.2–1.5 m) long. Bigeye and Pelagic Threshers display intra-uterine cannibalism.

94

The Thresher Shark can swim very fast. Sometimes it uses the huge, whiplike tail fin to propel its body clear of the surface in spectacular leaps. This behavior is most often seen when the shark is attempting to evade sports anglers.

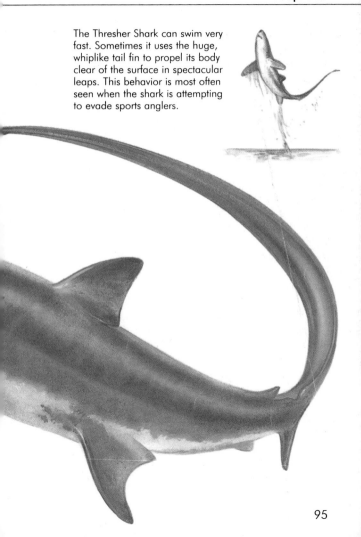

The family **Cetorhinidae** contains a single species, the Basking Shark. Highly migratory, it is found in all of the world's oceans. Like the Whale and Megamouth Sharks, the Basking Shark is a filter feeder. As with all Mackerel Sharks, the tail fin is almost symmetrical.

BASKING SHARK Cetorhinus maximus

Also called the Bone, Elephant, or Sailfish Shark, this is the world's second-largest fish after the Whale Shark. Extreme cases may grow to 49 feet (15 m), but 33 feet (10 m) is the usual limit. The Basking Shark lives in temperate waters of the Atlantic and Pacific. It seldom strays from continental shelves and is often seen in the surf. A gentle, slow swimmer, it spends a lot of time "basking" at the surface, often in large groups. During the winter, it stays close to the seabed.

The pectoral fins are large. The huge snout is pointed, and the jaws contain tiny, hooked teeth. The color may be dark blue, brownish, or charcoal gray above and paler below.

Cruising at the surface, the Basking Shark takes in huge amounts of plankton and small crustaceans. The female is thought to be ovoviviparous with oophagous embryos.

Caught for its flesh, oily liver, and fins, this species is highly endangered. It is now protected, with organizations around the world working for its long-term survival.

The Basking Shark
has enormous gill
slits. When not
feeding, the head
takes on a completely
different profile.

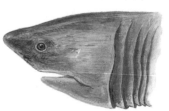

Sharing its name with the order, the Mackerel Shark family **Lamnidae** contains five species in three genera. Found worldwide, these big sharks are elegantly streamlined, with a spindle-shaped body and pointed snout. The gill slits are large. Uniquely among sharks, they can regulate their body temperature internally. They retain heat generated by the swimming muscles, which warms the blood, improving muscle strength and nervous activity.

All the lamnids are ovoviviparous, with some species displaying oophagy.

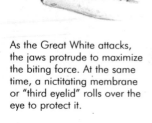

As the Great White attacks, the jaws protrude to maximize the biting force. At the same time, a nictitating membrane or "third eyelid" rolls over the eye to protect it.

GREAT WHITE SHARK *Carcharodon carcharias*

Also known as the White Death, White Pointer, and White Shark, this species grows to 23 feet (7.3 m). Usually a loner of shallow temperate waters, the Great White is found in every ocean. It is the most feared of all sharks, and though its true character is far from the avenging killer portrayed in the movie *Jaws*, it is one of the world's most advanced predators.

The body is spindle-shaped, with a blunt, conical snout. The first dorsal, pectoral, and tail fins are the main swimming fins. The 3,000 triangular, saw-edged teeth are up to 3 inches (7.5 cm) long and razor-sharp.

The Great White preys on anything from other fish to seabirds, seals, and small whales. Its acute senses help it track such victims from far afield.

The female gives birth to up to 14 pups. Heavily hunted, the Great White Shark is now a protected species.

99

The Mako makes spectacular leaps, clearing the water by up to 20 feet (6 m). This habit is often witnessed as an escape attempt when the Mako is hooked by sport anglers.

SHORTFIN MAKO *Isurus oxyrinchus*

This fast-swimming species is also known as the Mackerel, Snapper, or Bonito Shark, and as the Blue Pointer. It grows to 13 feet (4.3 m). A coastal and oceanic species of the Atlantic and Pacific, the Mako likes temperate and tropical waters above 61° F (16° C), ranging to depths of about 500 feet (150 m). This heat-seeker follows the warm water north in summer and south in winter.

The Mako has the spindle-shaped body characteristic of all the Mackerel Sharks, as well as large pectoral fins, a symmetrically lobed tail fin, and a large, erect first dorsal fin. The five gill slits are long. The body is metallic blue above and white below. The snout is long and the teeth are visible even when the mouth is closed.

Like most open-water sharks, the Mako eats practically anything it comes across – even items of little nutritional value. Favorite prey includes schooling fish, such as herring and mackerel; bluefish feature heavily in its inshore diet. Farther from land, it preys mainly on cephalopods. Larger Makos tackle billfish and even cetaceans.

Between 4 and 16 pups are born in a litter, having first eaten any unfertilized eggs in the uterus. The newborns measure about 2½ feet (70 cm) and grow rapidly. Males mature at about 6½ feet (2 m), females at a slightly greater length.

The upper and lower teeth are shaped like hooked daggers.

The Salmon Shark below is the cold-water equivalent of the Porbeagle. It is larger, but otherwise similar.

The teeth have sharply pointed cusps, ideal for grabbing fast-swimming prey. They lack the serrations seen in the Great White.

PORBEAGLE *Lamna nasus*

The Porbeagle or Mackerel Shark is the smallest of the lamnids, growing to 10 feet (3 m). It was classified with the almost identical Salmon Shark (*L. ditropis*) until 1947. The former is found in the relatively warm waters of the western Atlantic and south Pacific, while the Salmon Shark inhabits the colder waters of the North Pacific and the Bering Sea to Japan. The Porbeagle is found on continental shelves to depths of 1,200 feet (350 m), while its near relative prefers shallower waters down to 500 feet (120 m).

Like other lamnids, the Porbeagle has a stocky, spindle-shaped body. The first dorsal fin and pectorals are large, and the tail fin is crescent-shaped. Alone among sharks, the Porbeagle and Salmon Shark have an additional keel at each side of the tail tip, adding to their speed and power in the water.

In both species the snout is short and conical, the eyes fairly large, and the teeth sharp. The Porbeagle is bluish-gray with a paler underbelly. The hind tip of the large first dorsal fin is conspicuously white.

Both sharks prey on schooling fish such as mackerel and herrings; small sharks, including the tope and dogfish; and squid. The porbeagle also takes bottom-dwelling fish such as hake and flounder.

Both sharks are ovoviviparous. The embryos feed on unfertilized eggs and other embryos while in the uterus. Usually four pups are born, though sometimes only two, measuring 2½ feet (75 cm) in length.

The Porbeagle is heavily overfished, and with its low breeding rate is one of the most endangered shark species.

The order Carcharhiniformes (Ground Sharks) comprises 215 species in eight families. It is represented in all temperate and tropical waters. All Ground Sharks have an anal fin, two dorsal fins, and a long snout.

The 103 or more species in the family **Scyliorhinidae** (Catsharks) are sinuous sharks with catlike eyes. They occur in temperate and tropical waters to depths of over 6,500 feet (2,000 m). The first, spineless dorsal fin is usually small. The tail fin usually has a large lower lobe, and there are large spiracles.

CORAL CATSHARK *Atelomycterus marmoratus*

This striking-looking shark grows to a length of 2 feet (60 cm). It is often found on shallow inshore reefs in tropical and temperate waters of the Indian Ocean and western Pacific. It has the typically slender, flexible body of a Catshark, with a small tail fin.

Resting among corals by day, this shark hunts at night, snaking easily between the tightly packed coral heads and rocks in pursuit of invertebrates and bony fish.

Long labial grooves extend from the corners of the mouth, which almost join the nasal flaps.

The female Coral Catshark is oviparous, laying two eggs at a time. The purse-shaped egg cases have long tendrils, which help them anchor onto the seabed for the duration of their development. When the pups hatch, they measure just 4 inches (10 cm) in length. Females reach maturity at about five times this length.

SWELLSHARK *Cephaloscyllium ventriosum*

One of the largest Catsharks, the Swellshark grows to 3½ feet (1 m). It is one of seven species in a genus known for their defensive tactic of gulping water and puffing up the body until it is wedged firmly among rocks.

When distressed, a Swellshark gulps down mouthfuls of water to inflate its body. In doing so, it becomes wedged among rocks, stopping would-be predators from dislodging it.

This species lives in the subtropical eastern Pacific, from California to Mexico and Chile, in a depth range of 30–200 feet (9–60 m). It favors rocky areas and kelp beds.

The snout is broad and rounded. The two small dorsal fins are also rounded, and lie far back on the body. The tail fin is long, as in all of the Catsharks, and has a deep notch. The skin is studded with sharp denticles (toothlike scales).

The superbly camouflaged body is yellow-brown with dark blotches and saddlelike bars. The undersides and flanks are paler, with small dark brown spots.

Usually nocturnal, the Swellshark may rest with others in a group during the day. Swellsharks have been found piled in heaps, perhaps to appear larger to would-be predators. Small, sharp teeth help the shark catch small bony fish and crustaceans, which it ambushes from dark coral crevices.

The female lays two large egg cases at a time among plants. The pups hatch after 7–10 months, the period of development depending on the water temperature.

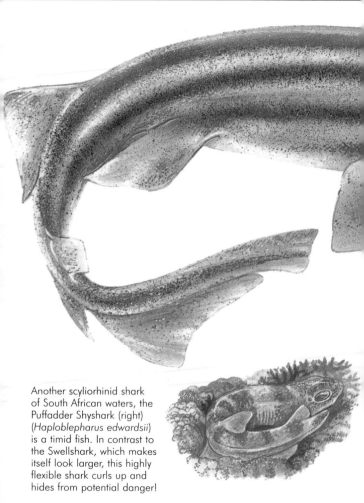

Another scyliorhinid shark of South African waters, the Puffadder Shyshark (right) (*Haploblepharus edwardsii*) is a timid fish. In contrast to the Swellshark, which makes itself look larger, this highly flexible shark curls up and hides from potential danger!

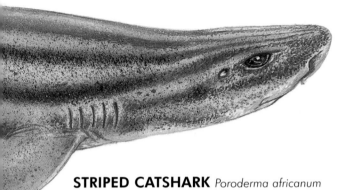

STRIPED CATSHARK *Poroderma africanum*

Also known as the Pyjama Catshark, this species can grow to a maximum length of 3⅓ feet (1 m). One of five *Poroderma* species, this common bottom-dweller is recognizable by its long, black body stripes. Endemic to South African waters, it is found in coastal shallows to depths of 300 feet (90 m).

The body is quite stout and the tail fin relatively short. On the middle fold of the nasal flap is a pair of short barbels which terminate before the mouth.

Active at night, the Striped Catshark lurks in caves or rock crevices during the day. The diet consists mainly of seabed crustaceans, such as crabs and shrimps, but also includes fish, cephalopods, and mollusks.

The female bears two tendriled egg cases. The pups that emerge 5–6 months later measure 6 inches (15 cm).

Though found only in a highly populated area that is heavily fished, the Striped Catshark is not currently under direct threat, but its status may be a cause for concern as international demand for shark meat increases.

SMALLSPOTTED CATSHARK *Scyliorhinus canicula*

Also called the Lesser Spotted Dogfish, this small shark may grow to 3⅓ feet (1 m) in length. Native to temperate waters of the northeastern Atlantic, it is found on continental shelves to depths of around 300 feet (90 m). A bottom-dweller, it favors mud and sand seabeds, but is found also in rocky areas.

Long and slender, the Smallspotted Catshark has two dorsal fins; the smaller second fin is set far back. There are five pairs of gill slits, with the hindmost two over the pectoral fins. The pale, tawny body has a sprinkling of small dark spots. Large eyes protrude slightly from the sides of the flattened head.

A placid shark, the Smallspotted Catshark rests during the day. At night it preys on small fishes, mollusks, and a variety of crustaceans. It also takes cephalopods and polychaete worms.

Female Catsharks gather in shallow inshore waters in the winter and are joined by males in the spring. In late summer the group migrates to deeper water to mate. Tendriled egg cases are laid two at a time in shallows. The pups hatch nine months later, measuring 3.5 inches (10 cm).

The female shark can lay as many as six eggs a week during the November–July breeding season.

110

Large nasal flaps extend back to the margins of this Catshark's mouth. There are no sensitive barbels.

The Finback Catsharks, family **Proscylliidae**, are small, elongate species favoring deeper waters to 2,300 feet (700 m). The first dorsal fin is set in front of the pelvic fins, rather than behind as in the true Catsharks.

Species include the Harlequin Catshark (*Ctenacis fehlmanni*), the Cuban Ribbontail Catshark (*Eridacnis barbouri*), the Pygmy ribbontail (*E. radcliffei*), the African Ribbontail (*E. sinuans*), and the Graceful Catshark.

GRACEFUL CATSHARK *Proscyllium habereri*

This shark, up to 26 inches (57 cm) long, lives in warm zones of the western Pacific, from southern Japan to Vietnam and Indonesia at depths of 150–300 feet (45–90 m).

Large, blackish spots mark the tan upperparts and stray onto the paler underside. The snout is long and pointed, and behind each catlike eye is a large spiracle. The long mouth contains tiny teeth.

A little-known bottom-dweller, this species probably eats small fishes, seabed crustaceans, and cephalopods. The female is believed to lay two eggs at a time, even though all other known proscyllids bear live young.

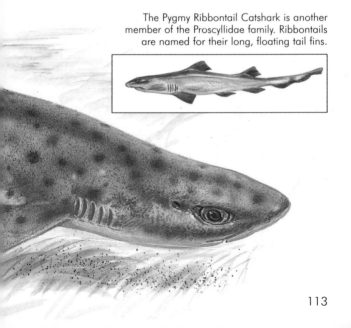

The Pygmy Ribbontail Catshark is another member of the Proscylliidae family. Ribbontails are named for their long, floating tail fins.

The family **Pseudotriakidae**, commonly known as the False Catsharks, contains only two species. Each is placed in its own genus.

False Catsharks are large, slender-bodied sharks. They are distinguished by the first dorsal fin, which is long and low and lacks the peak common in most sharks. These two sharks have a widespread distribution, keeping mainly to colder waters on insular and continental shelves at depths of 660–5,000 feet (200–1,500 m). They are the largest of all the carcharhiniform sharks.

The two species are the Slender Smoothhound (*Gollum attenuatus*) and the False Catshark described here.

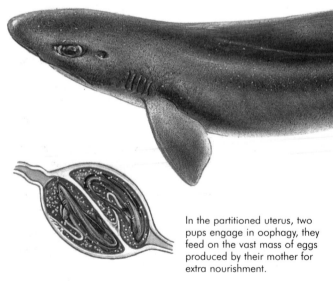

In the partitioned uterus, two pups engage in oophagy, they feed on the vast mass of eggs produced by their mother for extra nourishment.

FALSE CATSHARK *Pseudotriakis microdon*

Also known as the Dumb Shark, this species can reach lengths of 12 feet (3.5 m). It is patchily but widely distributed, occurring from Icelandic waters east to Indonesia.

Coloration is dark gray to dark brown, though the fins have darker margins. The mouth is long, with 200 rows of tiny teeth on each jaw. The first dorsal fin is characteristically low and sleek in profile. The second dorsal almost mirrors the anal fin, and the tail fin is weak.

The soft, fleshy body ideally suits this shark's sedentary lifestyle, spent preying on the deepwater fish and invertebrates that share its dark domain.

Although its breeding behavior is much debated, the female False Catshark is known to produce a vast number of eggs – more than 20,000 have been recorded. This huge overproduction (for a shark) may serve as a source of nourishment for fertilized pups, of which no more than four are ultimately born in each litter. This behavior makes the False Catshark one of only two sharks outside the Mackerel Sharks to exhibit oophagy, the other being the Tawny Nurse Shark.

Leptochariidae, the fourth family in the Ground Shark order Carcharhiniformes, contains just one species: the Barbeled Houndshark.

The common name alludes to the short, slender barbels that hang from beneath the nostrils. Aside from that feature, the Barbeled Houndshark is similar to the true Houndsharks of the family Triakidae and to the Finback Sharks of the family Pseudotriakidae.

BARBELED HOUNDSHARK

Leptocharias smithii
This small shark, no more than 2¾ feet (83 cm) long, favors inshore waters off tropical West Africa, from Mauritania south to Angola. It rests on muddy seabeds at depths of 30–250 feet (9–76 m).

The upper body is a uniform gray to brown, while the belly is paler and the fins are often dark. Though the pectoral and first dorsal fins are large, the underdeveloped tail suggests that the Barbeled Houndshark lives a largely sedentary lifestyle.

Behind the rounded eyes are very small spiracles. The elongate mouth has long labial furrows at its corners, and both jaws are armed with many sharp teeth. The barbels hanging from the snout are modified nasal folds. They play an important role in detecting seabed and shore-dwelling crustaceans in muddy or dark conditions. This shark also eats small fish, including anchovies, sardines, gobies, and flatfish, as well as fish eggs. As a testament to our polluting ways, Houndsharks have been found with stomachs full of all manner of human garbage.

During the mating act, the male bites the female to keep her still. The male has especially large teeth in the front of his jaws, which he puts to this purpose. The female is viviparous. After a gestation of four months she gives birth to, usually seven fully formed pups, measuring 1 foot (30 cm) in length and able to hunt for themselves.

The **Triakidae** family, containing 38 species in nine genera, includes the Tope Sharks, Smoothhounds, and Houndsharks. They are small or medium-sized sharks with oval eyes and nasal flaps. The two dorsal fins are spineless. Triakids are mainly warm-temperate species, found close to coastal shores on or near the seabed.

TOPE SHARK *Galeorhinus galeus*

Also known as the Soupfin, School, or Vitamin Shark, this species may reach 6½ feet (2 m). It is native to the Atlantic and Pacific, and though it occasionally migrates 1,000 miles (1,600 km) or more, it usually stays close to rocky or sandy beds in waters no deeper than 165 feet (50 m).

The Tope Shark has a slender, bronze-gray body with a long, flattened, and pointed snout. The second dorsal fin is much smaller than the first. The pectoral fins are large, and the pelvic fins are mid-sized and broad. The tail fin has a large ventral lobe with a deep notch, which can create the illusion of a double tail during bursts of fast swimming.

An active hunter, the Tope Shark preys mainly on bony

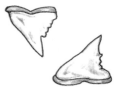

The teeth have sharp cusps, and on most of them the posterior edges are serrated, as shown here. Some have serrations on both edges.

fish, primarily codlike species and flatfish, although it also takes echinoderms and crustaceans.

The viviparous female reaches sexual maturity at about 10 years, at which time she is capable of pupping every two years. Gestation lasts a year, and she gives birth in the summer in shallow, inshore waters. Litters of around 20 pups are normal, although a large female can produce as many as 40. The lifespan may be up to 60 years.

A harmless species, the Tope Shark is fished not only for its meat, but also – as an alternative name implies – for its fin, in the barbaric practice of "finning". Numbers have dwindled significantly over the past 50 years, not helped by a naturally low reproductive rate, and now their conservation, with other finning victims, is at the forefront of international attention.

GUMMY SHARK *Mustelus antarcticus*

Also called the Australian Smoothhound, Flake, or Sweet William, this species may reach 5¾ feet (175 cm). It is native to the Indian Ocean and western Pacific off southern Australia and Tasmania, ranging to depths of 1,150 feet (350 m), but is capable of large migrations.

The bronze-gray body has a ridged back, and the snout is long and broad-tipped. The Gummy Shark may be seen in small schools of single-sex animals. The ovoviviparous female bears up to 40 young during the southern spring. The lifespan may exceed 16 years.

This species, now protected, has been heavily fished for its meat, which is known as "flake."

The jaws are broad and lined with flattened teeth, which are ideal for crunching tough crustaceans, as well as fish and cephalopods.

STARRY SMOOTHHOUND *Mustelus asterias*

Also called the Stellate Smoothhound or Gray Houndfish, this species may grow to 5 feet (1.4 m) in length. It occurs in the northeastern Atlantic, favoring sandy or gravelly beds at depths of up to 300 feet (90 m).

The pretty name derives from the white spots that adorn its dark body above the lateral line. It is a typical member of the Triakidae family, with large pectoral fins, a first dorsal fin that is larger than the second, and an elongate tail with a long lower lobe divided by a deep notch. The eyes are large and backed by large spiracles, and the snout is pointed and long.

Seabed crustaceans, including hermit crabs and lobsters, are the mainstay of the diet. The female matures at two or three years of age and is ovoviviparous, bearing a litter of 7 to 15 pups measuring 1 foot (30 cm).

An underview of this shark reveals the flattened underside. The pectoral and pelvic fins are winglike for sustained cruising.

LEOPARD SHARK *Triakis semifasciata*

The Leopard Shark may reach a length of 6 feet (2 m). This distinctive triakid is found off the Pacific coast of North America, from Oregon south to Baja California. It favors warm sandy, muddy, or coral shallows, seldom venturing deeper than 300 feet (90 m).

This shy shark tends to lie low, camouflaged by its beautiful markings. The skin is gray or bronze gray above and white below, overlaid with saddlelike stripes and blotches. The body is long and slender, with the back rising to a small hump at the first dorsal fin. The long tail has a notch in the upper fin. The oval-shaped eyes have nictitating membranes, the snout is long, and there are small spiracles directly behind the eyes.

The mouth lies below the pointed snout. There are pronounced flaps on the nostrils, but these have not developed into barbels.

Leopard sharks migrate annually in large groups along the coast. Their prey ranges from bony fish to shrimp, clams, crabs, and fish eggs, which they crush with small, pointed teeth.

The female gives birth during April and May to a litter of between 4 and 30 young, which measure 8 inches (20 cm).

This attractive and gregarious shark was once an abundant species, but is now becoming less so as a result of sport and commercial fishing. It is especially vulnerable on its annual migrations.

The Snaggletooth, named for its protruding lower teeth, is the largest member of the Weasel Shark family.

The Weasel Shark family **Hemigaleidae** contains seven species in four genera: *Chaenogaleus* (*C. macrostoma*), *Hemigaleus* (*H. microstoma*), *Hemipristis* (*H. elongatus*), and *Paragaleus* (*P. leucomatus*, *P. pectoralis*, *P. randalli*, and *P. tengi*).

These fairly common coastal species range to depths of 300 feet (90 m). All save one (described below) are confined to the continental Indo-West Pacific. Weasel Sharks are strong swimmers with two medium-sized, spineless dorsal fins and an anal fin. The tail fin has a strong lower lobe. The large eyes are oval in shape.

ATLANTIC WEASEL SHARK *Paragaleus pectoralis*

This species, which grows to 4½ feet (1.4 m), is the only Weasel Shark native to the eastern Atlantic. Found in warm waters off Africa, from Mauritania to Namibia, it ranges from the surf zone to depths of about 300 feet (90 m).

The first dorsal fin is larger than the second; the pectorals are long and pointed; and the anal fin can be slightly larger than the pelvic fins. The tail fin has a sharply pointed lower lobe. Overall coloring is pale gray to bronze above, with thin yellow stripes extending from the tail to the long, pointed snout. The belly is white. Short barbels hang from the nostrils, and the narrow jaws are packed with serrated teeth.

This species is a specialist predator of cephalopods (e.g. squid), but also eats bony fish. Like all hemigaleids, the female is viviparous, bearing up to four pups in a litter.

125

The family **Carcharhinidae** contains some of the best-known sharks – and some of the most feared. They are the Requiem or Whaler Sharks. There are 57 or more species in the family. Most are large and conform to the popular notion of how a "typical" shark looks. They have five paired gill slits, large eyes equipped with nictitating membranes, and large, erect fins. The body is typically spindle-shaped. Requiem Sharks are strong swimmers, and almost all have single-cusped, bladelike teeth. The family has a global distribution. Reproductive methods vary, but most species are viviparous.

BLACKTIP REEF SHARK *Carcharhinus melanopterus*

Also known as the Blacktip Shark or Guliman, this stocky species grows to a maximum 6 feet (1.8 m). It is common in shallow lagoons and coral reefs of the tropical Indo-Pacific and Mediterranean. It is able despite its bulk to swim in water only 1 foot (30 cm) deep, and seldom ventures beyond depths of 250 feet (75 m).

Not to be confused with the Blacktip Shark (page 136), this species is recognisable by its bold black-tipped fins. The first dorsal fin is erect and triangular; the smaller second fin is raked. The two are often seen breaking the water's surface. A sizable anal fin mirrors the second dorsal fin. The large tail fin has a deep subterminal notch

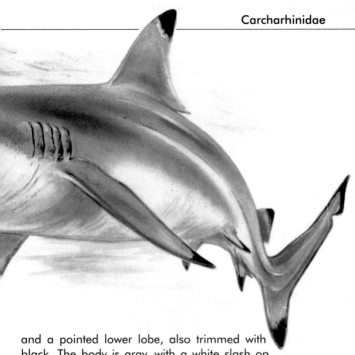

and a pointed lower lobe, also trimmed with black. The body is gray, with a white slash on the hindpart of each flank. The belly is pale.

The snout is pointed, and the wide, underslung mouth is armed with serrated, daggerlike teeth. These are primarily used in catching bony fish, but crustaceans and mollusks are also on the menu. The female bears two to four young, measuring 18 inches (45 cm).

This is another persecuted species, though it is not in immediate danger of decline. Its fins are sought for soup in Asia. The liver is utilized for its rich squalene content. The Blacktip is not a dangerous shark, though it has bitten reckless swimmers and divers in shallow water.

SILVERTIP SHARK *Carcharhinus albimarginatus*

The Silvertip Shark or Silver Whaler can reach 10 feet (3 m) in length. It inhabits shallow inshore reefs and shelves of the western Indian Ocean, as well as western and east-central parts of the Pacific.

The species is named for the white margins of its fins, which appear silver in the water. The first dorsal fin and the triangular pectoral fins are large. The others are small, with the exception of the strong tail fin. The body is gray-brown above and white below. The snout has a rounded tip, the eyes are small and round, and there are no spiracles.

The silvertip hunts reef-dwelling bony fish, such as wrasse, and larger open-water fish, such as tuna. The female is viviparous. After a 12-month gestation period she gives birth to five or six pups measuring 2 feet (60 cm).

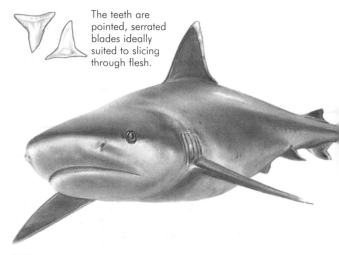

The teeth are pointed, serrated blades ideally suited to slicing through flesh.

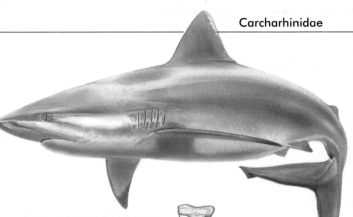

GRAY REEF SHARK

Carcharhinus amblyrynchos

Also known as the Long-nosed Blacktail, Black-Vee, or Whaler Shark, this species

The pointed, triangular teeth are blade-like with finely serrated edges.

may grow to 6 feet (2 m) in length. One of the most common Indo-Pacific shelf and reef sharks, it is found in large groups during the day in atoll passes and lagoons.

Like other Requiems, the Gray Reef Shark has a fusiform body. Coloring is dark-gray to bronze above, white below. The posterior margin of the tail fin is black, and some individuals have a white-tipped first dorsal fin.

Chiefly a nocturnal hunter, this shark preys on bony fish, squid, lobsters, and shrimps; sometimes in a "feeding frenzy", when it may become dangerous to people.

After a 12-month gestation period, the female bears up to six pups measuring 20 inches (50 cm). Although this shark is widespread, increasing unmanaged fishing in its specialized habitat is placing it under threat.

COPPER SHARK *Carcharhinus brachyurus*

Also known as the Bronze Whaler or Copper Requiem, this large shark may grow to 11 feet (3.3 m) in length. It inhabits temperate and tropical waters of the Atlantic and Pacific, from the surface to depths of about 300 feet (90 m). It is found in brackish as well as marine waters.

The spindle-shaped body is gray to bronze above and white below. On some individuals the pectoral and pelvic fins have dark tips. The tail fin has a pointed, lower lobe and a keeled upper lobe. The snout is bluntly rounded, and there are no spiracles behind the small eyes.

The Copper Shark preys mainly on bony fish, cephalopods, and small sharks and rays. The female is viviparous, bearing a litter of 13 to 20 pups which measure up to 28 inches (67 cm) long.

The teeth are pointed and serrated. Those in the upper jaw have strongly raked cusps.

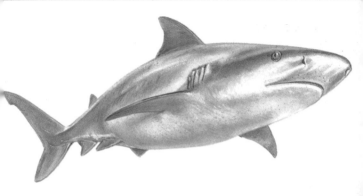

NERVOUS SHARK *Carcharhinus cautus*

Also called the Nervous Requiem, this species may grow to 4½ feet (1.5 m). It lives on tropical reefs of the Indo-western Pacific, from New Guinea to northern Australia.

The spindle-shaped body rises in a hump at the first dorsal fin, which is large. The tail base is keeled, and the upper tail fin is strongly notched. As with other Requiems the pelvic, anal, and second dorsal fin are much reduced.

The body is gray to light brown above and paler below, with a white flash along the flanks. The dorsal, caudal, and pectoral fins have black margins.

This shark of the shallows tends to shun deep water – hence its name. It preys on small fishes and crabs. The female is probably viviparous, like others of the family. The pups measure 16 inches (40 cm) at birth.

131

SILKY SHARK *Carcharhinus falciformis*

This migrant species, which may reach 11 ½ feet (3.5 m), is found in tropical waters worldwide. It lives in the open seas, from the surface to depths in excess of 1,500 feet (460 m).

Uniquely among carcharhinids, the first dorsal fin starts behind the pectoral fin's trailing edges. The pelvic and anal fins are reduced, and the lower lobe of the tail fin is triangular and stiff. The body is a uniform bluish gray above and white below.

The Silky Shark preys mostly on fish, such as tuna, as well as cephalopods and crabs. The females gives birth to between 2 and 14 pups per litter. An abundant and fairly aggressive shark, it is fished for the table. The skin also is used for leather products.

Fearsome, serrated teeth with slanted cusps line the small jaws. This shark can pose a danger to humans if provoked.

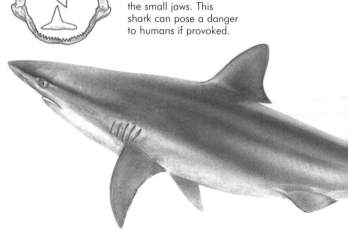

GALAPAGOS SHARK *Carcharhinus galapagensis*

This shark can grow to 12 feet (3.6 m). Despite the name, it is found – albeit patchily – in tropics worldwide, mainly off oceanic islands. It favors clear water around reefs, where adults range to depths of 600 feet (180 m) or more. A tell-tale feature of this stocky species is a ridge between the dorsal fins. Coloration is a dull gray to brown above, with a paler belly.

Preying mainly on squid and seabed fishes, the Galapagos shark also tackles sea lions. The female gives birth to as many as 16 pups measuring 30 inches (76 cm). The species may be potentially dangerous to humans.

The gape is broad and squarish, and the jaws bear the triangular, serrated teeth typical of this genus.

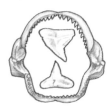

BULL SHARK *Carcharhinus leucas*

The many names for this impressive shark – the Cub, Ganges Shark, Nicaragua Shark, River Shark, Shovelnose, Slipway Gray, Square-nose, Van Rooyens, Zambezi Shark, Freshwater Whaler – testify to its widespread notoriety. Females can reach 12 feet (3.6 m), males 7 feet (2.3m).

This is an inshore species of all tropical and subtropical seas and oceans, and even enters fresh water in search of food. Its proximity to humans accounts for the many attacks recorded. It will even eat human corpses.

Behind the stubby snout the heavy body rises steeply to the large, erect first dorsal fin. The pectoral fins are also large and triangular, with pointed tips. The belly is creamy

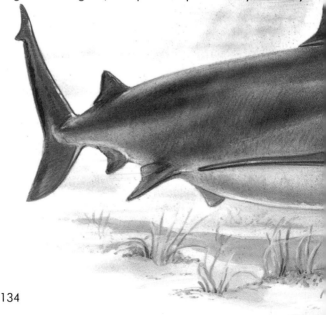

in color and the upper body gray. In juveniles the tail, pelvic, anal, and second dorsal fin have dark edges. There are small, round eyes, with no spiracles.

A hunter of bony fish in fresh water, the Bull Shark preys on other sharks, such as the Sandbar Shark, in the ocean. It also takes seabirds, turtles, cetaceans, and crustaceans. Up to 13 pups are born 10–12 months after a summer mating. This awesome shark is prized by anglers, though as an inshore dweller, it makes an easy catch.

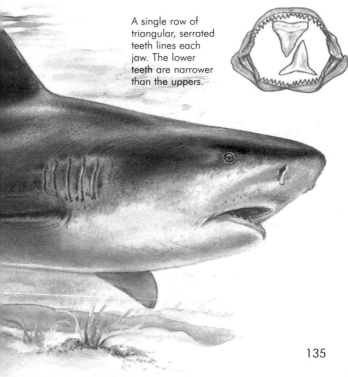

A single row of triangular, serrated teeth lines each jaw. The lower teeth are narrower than the uppers.

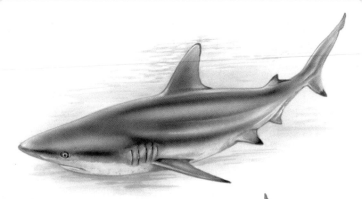

BLACKTIP SHARK

Carcharhinus limbatus

The Blacktip or Volador, which can reach a length of 8 feet (2.5 m), is found worldwide, though it favors waters off warm-temperate or tropical oceanic islands. This shark also visits mangrove swamps, muddy bays, and lagoons, and even freshwater habitats. It often joins large groups near the surface, and seldom dives deeper than 100 feet (30 m).

All the fins of this large, gray shark bear black tips, except the tail fin. The snout is pointed and rises directly from its tip to the large, first dorsal fin. Double rows of long, narrow teeth line the jaws.

The Blacktip speedily pursues bony fish including sardine, herring, anchovy, mackerel, and grouper, as well as other cartilaginous fish and crustaceans. The female is ovoviviparous, bearing up to 10 pups every two years after a 10–12-month gestation period.

136

LEMON SHARK *Negaprion brevirostris*

Reaching a maximum length of 11 feet (3.4 m), the Lemon Shark is a common species of the continental Atlantic and the eastern Pacific, from California to Equador. It is found mainly in reef waters to depths of 300 feet (90 m). Another species, the Sicklefin Lemon Shark, lives in the Indo-Pacific.

The Lemon Shark is named for its brownish-yellow color. Unlike the carcharhinids described so far, it has equal-sized dorsal fins. The snout is rounded and broad, and the wide jaws contain two rows of narrow, pointed teeth.

A lone hunter, the Lemon Shark preys on bony fish, such as mullet, grouper, and ladyfish. It is a potentially dangerous species, having been involved in attacks on humans in shallow water.

The ovoviviparous Lemon Shark gives birth to up to 18 pups, tail first. They measure 24 inches (60 cm).

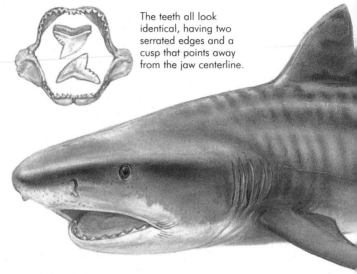

The teeth all look identical, having two serrated edges and a cusp that points away from the jaw centerline.

TIGER SHARK *Galeocerdo cuvier*

The Tiger Shark may grow to 24 feet (7.3 m). One of the most revered of all sharks, it occurs in all tropical waters of the world's oceans. A solitary oceanic nomad, it stays in deep waters during the day, moving closer inland to feed.

The "tiger" stripes are at their strongest on young or small sharks, which also have dark spots on their pale fins. The stripes fade to a mottled appearance in adults, which are bluish to gray above and yellowish white below.

The snout is blunt. A ridge runs between the two dorsal fins, the first of which is larger. The large pectorals are broad and round-tipped. The powerful tail fin is pointed above, with a raked lower lobe. All told, the body and fin arrangement make this a terrifically powerful predator.

The Tiger Shark's natural diet features other sharks and rays, bony fish, and occasionally aquatic mammals, as well as sea snakes, turtles, lobsters, crabs, and conch. However, this marauder eats whatever fits inside its mouth, including other Tiger Sharks! Unusual stomach contents have included beer bottles, potatoes, dogs, deer antlers, car licenses, and even a chicken coop – complete with feathers. With its fearsome teeth and unfussy diet, the Tiger Shark deserves its nickname as the goat of the ocean.

There is a belief that poor eyesight accounts for the Tiger Shark's random diet. Its vision is, however, excellent – as is its sense of smell, which detects even the faintest trace of blood, animal or human, in the water.

The female is ovoviviparous. After a gestation of usually nine months, she gives birth to up to 80 pups, measuring up to 30 inches (75 cm). Surprisingly perhaps, this species has little commercial value and is largely ignored by fisheries.

BLUE SHARK *Prionace glauca*

Also known as the Blue Whaler, Great Blue Shark, or Blue Dog, this sleek species can reach 12½ feet (3.9 m). It has probably the widest distribution of any shark, found in the three major oceans. It migrates long distances to remain in temperatures in the range of 55–65° F (13–18° C). In the tropics it stays deep, to 1,150 feet (350 m) or so; in temperate regions it prefers surface waters.

The deep indigo of the upper body, from which the shark earns its name, fades to a paler, brighter blue on the flanks, and the belly is paler still. The distinctive snout is long and rounded at the tip, and the eyes are large and round with a white rim. The pectoral fins are unusually long and pointed. As in other Requiem sharks the pelvic, anal, and second dorsal fins are reduced. The first dorsal fin is

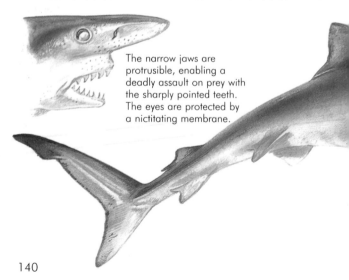

The narrow jaws are protrusible, enabling a deadly assault on prey with the sharply pointed teeth. The eyes are protected by a nictitating membrane.

triangular and large, with a free trailing edge at the root. Unlike many other carcharhinids, there is no interdorsal ridge, although visible keels flank the base of the long tail. The asymmetric tail fin has a pronounced notch. The jaws are long and narrow and are lined with long, narrow and sharply serrated teeth.

The Blue Shark is an extremely graceful, solitary cruiser, opportunistically attacking bony fish such as herring, mackerel, sardines, and anchovies, as well as squid.

The male matures at about four years of age, the female at about five. She is viviparous, and after a gestation period of 9–12 months she normally bears between 25 and 50 pups, though litters of more than 130 have been reported.

A common species subject to no commercial fishing, the Blue Shark is prized as a game fish. They have a chilling reputation for homing in on dead cetaceans and human disaster victims at sea.

WHITETIP REEF SHARK *Triaenodon obesus*

Also known as the Blunthead Shark, this species can reach a length of 7 feet (2.1 m). It is widespread across the Indo-Pacific. A bottom-dweller, it seldom surfaces, though it remains close to inshore coral reefs in clear waters no deeper than 130 feet (40 m). Sometimes several Whitetips amass in heaps inside coral caves.

Long and slender, the Whitetip has a second dorsal fin almost equal in size to the first, and the anal fin is also largish. The broad head has a blunt snout with noticeable nasal flaps. The large eyes have vertical pupils. The body is dark gray to brown above and pale below, and the dorsal and tail fins have white tips.

The teeth are mid-sized and, uniquely, have three cusps. This adaptation enables the shark to tug lodged prey out of coral crevices. It hunts mainly small fish, but also has a taste for octopus. The Whitetip may also jam its body into coral crevices in pursuit of prey, thrashing its body wildly to tear a bite-sized chunk from its victims.

The viviparous female bears up to five pups, each up to 24 inches (60 cm) long, after a 13-month gestation period. The species is not in danger, nor considered dangerous to humans.

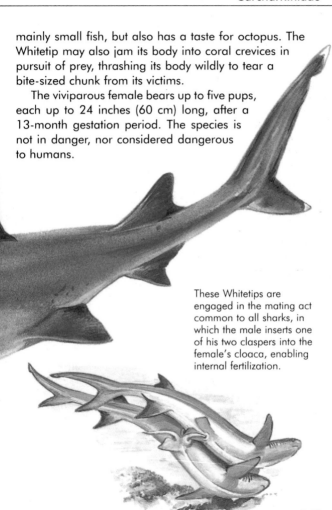

These Whitetips are engaged in the mating act common to all sharks, in which the male inserts one of his two claspers into the female's cloaca, enabling internal fertilization.

143

This extraordinary-looking family of sharks are the **Sphyrnidae**, the suitably named Hammerhead Sharks. There are nine species classified in two genera. The first genus, *Eusphyra*, contains a single species, the Winghead Shark (*E. blochii*). The second genus, *Sphyrna*, contains the remaining eight hammerheads.

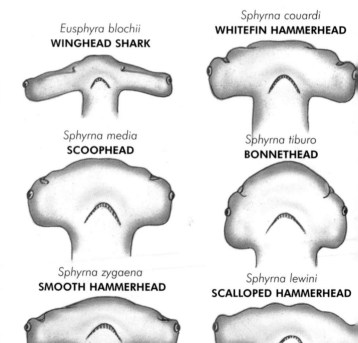

Eusphyra blochii
WINGHEAD SHARK

Sphyrna couardi
WHITEFIN HAMMERHEAD

Sphyrna media
SCOOPHEAD

Sphyrna tiburo
BONNETHEAD

Sphyrna zygaena
SMOOTH HAMMERHEAD

Sphyrna lewini
SCALLOPED HAMMERHEAD

The feature evidently common to all these sharks is the flattening and lateral expansion of the snout into a structure known as a cephalofoil (literally "head wing"). The large eyes are located at the ends of this structure. Aside from the odd head shape, hammerheads are similar to members of the family Carcharhinidae.

Sphyrna corona
SCALLOPED BONNETHEAD

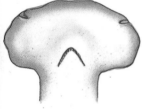

Sphyrna tudes
SMALLEYE HAMMERHEAD

Sphyrna mokarran
GREAT HAMMERHEAD

Most hammerheads live in warm coastal and offshore waters, ranging from the surface to depths of about 900 feet (275 m). None live at the seabed or in very deep waters, nor are any oceanic.

Hammerheads have a habit, while swimming, of swaying the head from side to side. This may enable the electrosensory organs to function at their best, or simply improve their vision. Some hammerhead species are often observed in large groups. Gatherings of more than 500 occur at feeding sites, where the sharks may collectively feed.

The nine species of Hammerhead Shark can be identified by their head shape and snout profile.

145

GREAT HAMMERHEAD SHARK

Sphyrna mokarran

Also known as the Scoop Hammerhead, this shark grows to a maximum length of 20 feet (6 m). It is found in almost all tropical and warm-temperate waters, close to coasts. It ventures into open waters, usually at the surface, and to depths of 260 feet (80 m). Highly nomadic, they migrate towards the poles in summer.

The body is slender and long. The first dorsal fin is tall. The upper lobe of the tail fin is long and pointed, with a hooked keel near the tip. The pectorals are long and triangular, and the large anal fin is much longer than the second dorsal. The brow of the snout is fairly straight, except for a central indentation. The body is bronze gray above, with a paler underside.

The Great Hammerhead is one of the largest sharks, and is a voracious predator. It takes a range of bony fish, as well as other sharks and rays – especially stingrays.

Reproduction is viviparous, the female bearing between 5 and 40 pups, measuring 2 feet (60 cm), after an 11-month gestation period.

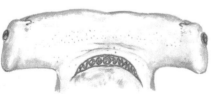

The broad "hammer," laden with sensors, may help this shark scan seabeds in search of concealed stingrays – apparently a favorite prey.

146

SHARK COUSINS

The Chondrichthyes class of cartilaginous fish comprises two subclasses: Elasmobranchii, the sharks and rays, and Holocephalii, the chimeras.

Rays includes the skates, electric torpedo rays, stingrays, sawfishes, eagle rays, and manta rays, among others. They are collectively known as batoids.

Batoids are thought to have branched off from the shark lineage during the age of the dinosaurs. Their separate specialization is likely to have been associated with their bottom-dwelling lifestyle. The bottom-dwelling sharks evolved some time after the batoids and are the result of convergent evolution.

The growth of the batoids saw an expansion of pectoral fins and a reduction in tails, especially in the rays and skates. These physical modifications for sluggish seabed living contrast with the adaptations for speed, power, and agility adopted by modern oceanic sharks. Rays and skates further diverged from most sharks in becoming flatter. This flattening is seen also in the Angelsharks and Wobbegongs, which inhabit the same niche as the rays. Unlike the seabed sharks, the rays and skates have enlarged pectoral fins, which are fused to the head and extend toward the tail, comprising what is called the "disc". (In the Angelsharks and Wobbegongs the pectorals remain separate from the head.) The large pectorals enable batoids to swim almost as though in flight, and their fins are referred to as "wings."

Batoids also differ from sharks in their breathing apparatus. Their five paired gill slits open on the underside of the body. This adaptation enables rays to breathe easily on the seabed. Water enters through spiracles on top of the head and is expelled through the gills on their underside.

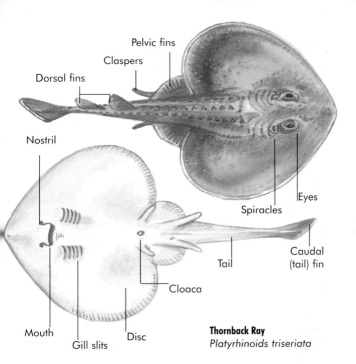

Thornback Ray
Platyrhinoids triseriata

Labels: Pelvic fins, Claspers, Dorsal fins, Nostril, Mouth, Gill slits, Disc, Cloaca, Tail, Spiracles, Eyes, Caudal (tail) fin

Batoids range widely in size. One stingray is just 16 inches (40 cm) long, while the pectoral fins of a manta ray can span 23 feet (7 m)! Batoids are also diverse in their breeding methods. Most rays are ovoviviparous. Skates are oviparous; their empty egg cases, popularly known as "mermaids' purses," wash up on beaches in the fall.

There are more than 550 batoid species. Some experts place all the batoids in one big order, Rajiformes, while others split them into several orders (of which Rajiformes is just one). This book follows the latter arrangement.

SKATES Rajiformes

There are more than 250 species of skate in a single family, Rajidae. Most have a lozenge-shaped pectoral disc that is divided from the tail. There are one or two dorsal fins, a variable tail fin, and large denticles (tooth-like scales) in the skin, usually extending down the back.

Most skate species are marine, ranging from inshore shallows to soft seabeds at depths of 8,000 feet (2,750 m) or more. They typically eat seabed crustaceans and fish.

ELECTRIC RAYS Torpediniformes

There are about 70 species of electric ray in four families. Most are oval in outline, with loose skin and a developed tail bearing two dorsal fins and a caudal fin. The electrical discharges are produced by modified cells in the pectoral fins on each side of the head. Some species can produce shocks of almost 300 volts. Rays use their high-voltage equipment to stun attackers as a defensive tactic, or to stun prey for easy capture.

STINGRAYS Myliobatiniformes

There are some 180 species of stingray in 10 families. They are found in all warm tropical and subtropical waters of the world's oceans. Typically flattened in a disc or lozenge outline, they have a slim tail commonly reduced to a whip.

In place of fins, the tail bears one or two serrated spines. Each spine, which is a modified skin denticle, has a groove along the ventral surface which contains venom-producing tissues. If you are unfortunate enough to step on a stingray buried in tropical shallows, it whips its tail from side to side in an attempt to stab a spine into the offending foot. The effect of the venom is a painful throbbing, as well as acute localized pain. A deep wound to the chest, typically inflicted on unlucky divers, can occasionally result in death.

Lesser Electric Ray
Narcine brasiliensis

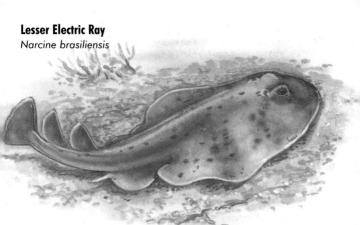

Ribbontail Stingray
Taeniura lymma

This species has two venomous spines near the tail tip.

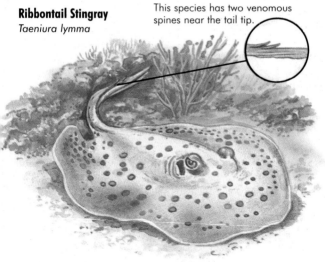

MANTA RAY Mobulidae

One of the largest, yet also one of the least known rays, this giant of the seas is found around the world in tropical waters. Although classified in the stingray order, the Manta (*Manta birostris*) is a stingless ray. It shares its family with the similar devilrays (*Mobula* ssp.), which differ in having a smaller terminal mouth.

The Manta Ray is found around inshore coastal waters, but is also one of the few pelagic-adapted rays – a ray equivalent, perhaps, of the Megamouth or Whale Shark.

Like these giant sharks, the Manta is a filter-feeder of plankton and small bony fishes. It directs food to its massive mouth with the aid of greatly enlarged cephalic lobes, which gather and scoop up prey into the mouth.

Cephalic lobes

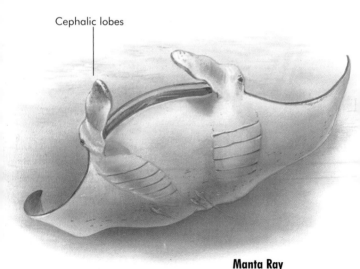

Manta Ray
Manta birostris

EAGLE RAYS Myliobatididae

There are around 24 recognized species of Eagle Ray. Like the Manta, they are found circumglobally, often in schools, in all warm-temperate and tropical seas. The body is broader than it is long, and the winglike pectorals are triangular. The tail is longer than the body and, unlike the Manta, bears one or two caudal spines.

Eagle Rays are found over muddy and sandy bottoms of coastal waters, bays, and estuaries. They have plates of crushing teeth and feed mainly on shrimps, crabs, gastropods, polychaete worms, and bony fish. They use their large pectoral wings to excavate their prey from the seabed or, conversely, to bury themselves in mud.

Spotted Eagle Ray
Aetobatus narinari

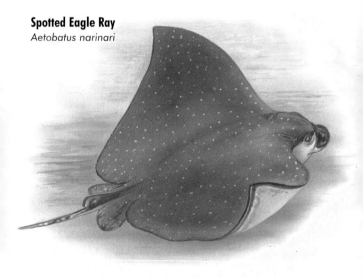

GUITARFISH Rhynchobatiformes

It is thought that these bizarre-looking fish represent an intermediate form between sharks and rays. There are two families of Guitarfish and about 44 species. They are found in all warm-temperate and tropical waters of the world.

A well-known species is the Atlantic Guitarfish. One of the Shovelnose Guitarfish, it ranges along the American seaboard from the Caribbean to southern Mexico, and can reach a length of 2½ feet (75 cm).

Guitarfish have characteristically flattened bodies, with the enlarged pectoral fins of rays but also with the dorsal fins, tail, and swimming method of sharks. The head is long, broad, and flattened, and the snout is pointed. The overall profile is reminiscent of a guitar body.

Atlantic Guitarfish
Rhinobatus lentiginosus

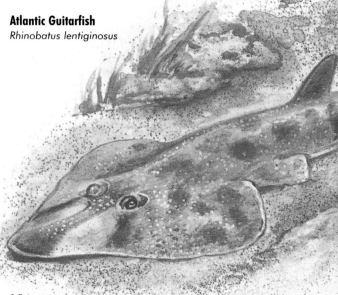

Smalltooth Sawfish
Pristis pectinata

SAWFISH Pristioformes

There are just six species of Sawfish, and they are unmistakable with their narrowly elongated, sawlike snout.

Sawfish inhabit a similar niche to the Sawsharks, which they superficially resemble. They differ from the sharks, however, in that their snout is edged with protruding, strongly embedded teeth, all of roughly equal size. Beyond the snout, however, the Sawfish body is typically sharklike.

Like the Sawsharks, the Sawfish use their specialized snout to disable or kill prey, and to dig up buried crustaceans and bivalve mollusks from the ocean floor.

155

CHIMERAS

The other subclass of the Chondrichthyes comprises the Holocephalii, or Chimeras, of which there are 35 species in three families. Also known as Ratfishes, Elephantfishes, or Ghostsharks, these odd-looking fish probably diverged from shark ancestors some 200 million years before the rays. Today they are found in cold and often deep waters of the world's tropical and temperate oceans. Normally found offshore, they occasionally venture near coasts.

Spotted Ratfish
Hydrolagus colliei

The typical Chimera has a large head, big eyes, and a curiously extended snout. It has a gill covering over the four gill slits per side, and lacks spiracles. The upper jaw is fixed to the skull, unlike the sharks, and the jaws contain only a few rabbitlike teeth: one pair in the upper jaw, and two pairs in the lower. The Chimera has no single cloaca; instead, it has separate anal and urogenital openings. In addition to his claspers, a male Chimera has an extra appendage on the head which helps him grip the female while mating.

INDEX

TAKE ACTION TO HELP SHARKS:

Sign the Shark Trust petition to ban shark finning and join the Shark Trust

see www.sharktrust.org